Foreword

As an education and training organization within the IT Service Management (ITSM) industry, we have been impressed by the positive changes introduced by the version 3 refresh of the ITIL® framework. The evolution of the core principles and practices provided by the framework provides the more holistic guidance needed for an industry that continues to mature and develop at a rapid pace. We recognize however, that many organizations and individuals who had previously struggled with their adoption of the framework will continue to find challenges in 'implementing' ITIL® as part of their approach for governance of IT Service Management practices. In light of this, one of our primary goals is to provide the quality education and support materials needed to enable the understanding and application of the ITIL® framework in a wide-range of contexts.

This comprehensive book is designed to complement the in-depth accredited eLearning ITIL® Foundation course provided by The Art of Service. The interactive eLearn course uses a combination of narrated PowerPoint presentations with flat text supplements and multiple choice assessments. This book provides added value to the eLearn course by providing additional text and real life examples to further cement your knowledge. Your learning and understanding will be maximized by combining these two study resources, which will ultimately prepare you for the APMG ITIL® Foundation certification exam. This edition has also included appropriate alterations based on recent changes to the ITIL V3 Foundation syllabus and the associated exams. We have also used taken customer feedback to make improvements to the material, including additional content and sample exam questions.

We hope you find this book to be a useful tool in your educational library and wish you well in you IT Service Management career!

The Art of Service

Write a review to receive any *free* eBook from our Catalog - $99 Value!

If you recently bought this book we would love to hear from you! Benefit from receiving a free eBook from our catalog at http://www.emereo.org/ if you write a review on Amazon (or the online store where you purchased this book) about your last purchase!

How does it work?

To post a review on Amazon, just log in to your account and click on the Create your own review button (under Customer Reviews) of the relevant product page. You can find examples of product reviews in Amazon. If you purchased from another online store, simply follow their procedures.

What happens when I submit my review?

Once you have submitted your review, send us an email at review@emereo.org with the link to your review, and the eBook you would like as our thank you from http://www.emereo.org/. Pick any book you like from the catalog, up to $99 RRP. You will receive an email with your eBook as download link. It is that simple!

How to access the eLearning Program

1. Direct your browser to: www.theartofservice.org
2. Click 'login' (found at the top right of the page)
3. Click 'Create New Account'
4. Follow the instructions to create a new account. You will need a valid email address to confirm your account creation. If you do not receive the confirmation email check that it has not been automatically moved to a Junk Mail or Spam folder.
5. Once your account has been confirmed, email your User-ID for your new account to key@theartofservice.com
6. You will receive a return email with an enrolment key that you will need to use in order to access the eLearning program. Next time you login to the site, access the program titled: *ITIL V3 Foundation eLearning Program*

Minimum system requirements for accessing the eLearning Program:

Processor   : Pentium 4 (1 GHz) or higher

RAM   : 256MB (512 MB recommended)

OS   : Windows XP, Vista, 7, MCE, Mac OSX

Browser   : Macromedia Firefox 3+ (recommended), Internet Explorer 6.x or higher, Safari, Opera, Chrome, all with cookies and JavaScript enabled.

Plug-Ins   : Adobe Flash Player 8 or higher

Internet Connection   : Due to multimedia content of the site, a minimum connection speed of 512kbs is recommended. If you are behind a firewall and are facing problems in accessing the course or the learning portal, please contact your network administrator for help

If you are experiencing difficulties with the Flash Presentations within the eLearning Programs please make sure that:

1) You have the latest version of Flash Player installed, by visiting

2) You check that your security settings in your web browser don't prevent these flash modules playing.

3) For users of Internet Explorer 7 a solution involves DESELECTING "Allow active content to run files on my computer" in Internet Explorer -->Tools, Options, Advanced, Security settings.

Contents

1 Introduction

Looking back on a year where corporate giants fell and government bailouts were measured in the billions, the challenges faced by a typical IT Service Provider may seem of low priority. But now that IT budgets have come under more financial scrutiny than ever before, the value provided by managing IT with controlled, repeatable and measurable processes has become all the more obvious. So for the modern Chief Information Officer (CIO), employing quality IT Service Management (ITSM) practices can often help in achieving a quality sleep each night.

The term IT Service Management is used in many ways by different management frameworks and the organizations that seek to use them. While there are variations across these different sources of guidance, common elements for defining ITSM include:

- Description of the **processes** required to deliver and support IT Services for customers.
- A focus on delivering and supporting the **technology or products** needed by the business to meet key organizational objectives or goals.
- Definition of roles and responsibilities for the **people** involved including IT staff, customers and other stakeholders involved.
- The management of **external suppliers (partners)** involved in the delivery and support of the technology and products being delivered and supported by IT.

The combination of these elements provide the capabilities required for an IT organization to deliver and support quality IT Services that meet specific business needs and requirements.

The official ITIL® definition of IT Service Management is found within the Service Design volume (page 11), describing ITSM as *"A set of specialized organizational capabilities for providing value to customers in the form of services"*. These organizational capabilities are influenced by the needs and requirements of customers, the culture that exists within the service organization and the intangible nature of the output and intermediate products of IT services.

However IT Service Management comprises more than just these capabilities alone, being complemented by an industry of professional practice and wealth of knowledge, experience and skills. The ITIL® framework has developed as a major source of good practice in Service Management and is used by organizations worldwide to establish and improve their ITSM practices.

1.1 The Four Perspectives (Attributes) of ITSM

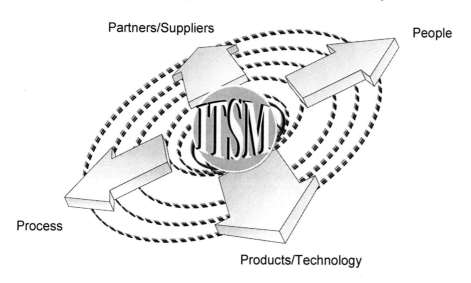

Figure 1.A – Four Perspectives (Attributes) of ITSM

There are four perspectives ("4P's") or attributes that are important to consider in order for IT Service Management to be successful.

Partners/Suppliers Perspective: Takes into account the importance of Partner and External Supplier relationships and how they contribute to Service Delivery. It will help to ensure that suppliers deliver value for money, and provide services that are clearly aligned to business requirements.

People Perspective: Concerned with the "soft" side of ITSM. This requires IT staff, customers and other stakeholders to understand the purpose of ITSM and how it should be used within the organization. Training and education should be provided to ensure staff members have the correct skills, knowledge and motivation to perform their roles.

Products/Technology Perspective: Takes into account the quality of IT services themselves, and all technology architectures (hardware & software) required to provision them. Technology should be leveraged to both support and drive strategic opportunities for the business.

Process Perspective: Relates the end-to-end delivery of services based on process flows. By having clearly established processes (with documentation, guidelines and other supporting tools), it will enable a more consistent, repeatable and measurable approach to the management of services.

Quality IT Service Management ensures that all of these four perspectives are taken into account as part of the continual improvement of the IT organization. It is the same when designing new or modified Services themselves, in that these four perspectives need to be considered and catered for in order to enable success in its design, transition and eventual use by customers.

1.2 Benefits of ITSM

While the benefits of applying IT Service Management practices vary depending on the organization's needs, some typical benefits include:

- Improved quality service provision
- Cost-justifiable service quality
- Design of services that meet business, customer and user demands
- Integrated and centralized processes
- Transparency of the roles and responsibilities for service provision
- Continual improvement, incorporating 'lessons learnt' into future endeavors
- Measurable quality, performance and efficiency attributes.

It is also important to consider the range of stakeholders who can benefit from improved ITSM practices. As perspectives will differ for each stakeholder, the benefits provided by enhanced ITSM practices may apply to one or more of the following parties:

- Senior management
- Business unit managers
- Customers
- End users
- IT staff
- Suppliers
- Shareholders.

1.3 Business and IT Alignment

A common theme in any IT Service Management framework is to enable and demonstrate business and IT alignment. When staff members of an IT organization have only an internal focus on the technology being delivered and supported, they lose sight of the actual purpose and benefit that their efforts deliver to the business and customers. A way in which to communicate how IT supports the business is using Figure 1.B (on the next page), demonstrating business and IT alignment.

Figure 1.B divides an organization into a number of supporting layers that work towards meeting a number of organizational goals. These layers are communicated by the following:

Organization: What are the key strategic goals and objectives for the organization? These objectives define who we are as an organization and where we want to be in the future.

CORE Business Processes: These are represented by the repeatable business activities that produce desirable results for the business. Without these results, the organizational objectives defined above would not be supported or achieved.

IT Service Organization: Defines the IT Services and supporting infrastructure that is required to enable the effective and efficient execution of the business processes above. IT Services are used by the business to facilitate and enhance outcomes, including improved efficiency of operations or ensuring accuracy in the records and information being managed.

IT Service Management: Made up by the repeatable, managed and controlled processes used by the IT department that enables quality and efficiency in the delivery and support of the IT Services above.

IT Technical Activities: The actual technical activities required as part of the execution of the ITSM processes above. ITSM is utilized to ensure that any resources and effort spent performing the technical activities are optimized according to the greatest business need or reward. As these activities are technology specific (e.g. configuring application server), they will not be a focus of this book's content.

Each layer within this structure is utilized to support the layer(s) above. At the same time, each layer will in some way influence the layer below them. For example, a business process that is required to be executed at all times without disruptions (e.g. emergency health services) would result in highly resilient IT services being implemented, supported by ITSM processes that reduce the risk and impact of disruptions occurring.

Our Business: A fashion store

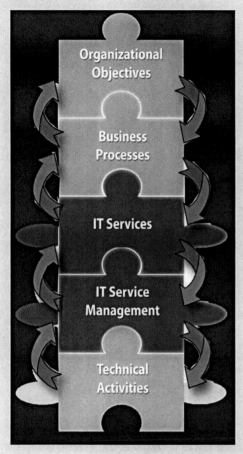

Figure 1.B – Business and IT Alignment

What are some of our organization's objectives or strategic goals?

- We want to increase profits by 15% each year
- We want to have a good image and reputation, with a loyal customer base.

What Business Processes aid in achieving those objectives?

- Retail/sales
- Marketing
- Manufacturing
- Procurement, HR, finance etc.

What IT Services are these business processes dependent on?

- Web sites (internal and external)
- Communication services (email, video conferencing)
- Automatic procurement system for buying products
- Point of Sale Services.

We have ITSM in order to make sure the IT Services are:

- What we need (Service Level Management, Capacity Management etc.)
- Available when we need it (Availability Management, Incident Management etc.)
- Provisioned cost-effectively (Financial Management, Service Level Management)

If we don't manage the IT Services appropriately we cannot rely on these services to be available when we need. If too many disruptions occur, we cannot adequately support our business processes effectively and efficiently. If the business processes are operating as they should, we will ultimately fail to support and achieve our overall organization's objectives!

Also note the relationship between IT Service Management processes and the technical activities below. Used properly, ITSM processes can optimize the time, effort and other resources spent performing technical activities, ensuring that all staff actions are working in accordance to agreed business priorities and objectives.

This is just a simple example used to illustrate the relationship between ITSM and the organization. Any approach used to improve ITSM practices should always be carefully considered to ensure that the plans suit the organization, in terms of:

- Size (number of staff, customers, IT devices etc.)
- Geographical dispersion
- Culture and ethos
- Current maturity and capability levels.

1.4 What is ITIL®?

ITIL® stands for the Information Technology Infrastructure Library. ITIL® is the international de facto management framework describing "good practices" for IT Service Management. The ITIL® framework evolved from the UK government's efforts during the 1980s to document how successful organizations approached service management. By the early 1990s they had produced a large collection of books documenting the "best practices" for IT Service Management. This library was eventually entitled the IT Infrastructure Library. The Office of Government Commerce in the UK continues to operate as the trademark owner of ITIL®.

ITIL® has gone through several evolutions and was most recently refreshed with the release of version 3 in 2007. Through these evolutions the scope of practices documented has increased in order to stay current with the continued maturity of the IT industry and meet the needs and requirements of the ITSM professional community.

ITIL® is only *one of many* sources for ITSM good practices, and should be used to complement any other set of practices being used by an organization.

Five volumes make up the IT Infrastructure Library (Version 3).

- Service Strategy
- Service Design
- Service Transition
- Service Operation
- Continual Service Improvement.

Each volume provides the guidance necessary for an integrated approach, and addresses capabilities' direct impact on a service provider's performance. The structure of the ITIL framework is that of the service lifecycle. It ensures organizations are able to leverage capabilities in one area for learning and improvements in others. The framework is used to provide structure, stability and strength to service management capabilities with durable principles, methods and tools. This enables service providers to protect investments and provide the necessary basis for measurement, learning and improvement.

In addition to the core publications there is also *ITIL Complimentary Guidance*. This consists of a complimentary set of publications with guidance specific to industry sectors, organization types, operating models and technology architectures. At present, this complimentary guidance is available by subscription from http://www.bestpracticelive.com.

1.4.1 Good practices

Ignoring public frameworks and standards can needlessly place an organization at a disadvantage. Organizations should seek to cultivate their own proprietary knowledge on top of a body of knowledge developed from using public frameworks and standards.

Public frameworks (ITIL, COBIT, CMMI etc.): Frameworks are scaled and adapted by the organization when implemented, rather than following a prescriptive set of practices (standards). Examples of public frameworks for ITSM include:

- ITIL ®.
- COBIT – The Control Objectives for Information and related Technology.
- Capability Maturity Model Integrated (CMMI) for IT Services.

Standards: Usually a formal document that establishes uniform engineering or technical criteria, methods, processes and practices. Unlike frameworks, they are prescriptive in declaring mandatory elements that must be demonstrated. Examples of standards relating to ITSM are:

- ISO/IEC 20000 – International Standard for IT Service Management.
- ISO/IEC 27001 – International Standard for Information Security Management Systems.

Proprietary knowledge of organizations and individuals: Specific expertise developed for internal purposes, or developed in order to sell to other organizations (e.g. Gartner).

Generally good practices are defined as those formalized as a result of being **successful in wide-industry use.**

2 Common Terminology

Critical to our ability to participate with and apply the concepts from the ITIL® framework is the need to be able to speak a common language with other IT staff, customers, end-users and other involved stakeholders. This chapter documents the important common terminology that is used throughout the ITIL® framework.

Care should be taken when attempting the ITIL Foundation exam, as there will be a number of questions that seek to ensure the candidate has an effective grasp of the terminology used throughout the framework.

Terminology	Explanations
IT Service Management:	A set of specialized organizational capabilities for providing value to customers in the form of services.
Capabilities:	The ability of an organization, person, process, application, CI or IT service to carry out an activity. Capabilities can be described as the functions and processes utilized to manage services. These are intangible assets of an organization that cannot be purchased, but must be developed and matured over time. The ITSM set of organizational capabilities aims to enable the effective and efficient delivery of services to customers.
Resources:	A generic term that includes IT Infrastructure, people, money or anything else that might help to deliver an IT service. Resources are also considered to be tangible assets of an organization.
Process:	A set of *coordinated activities* combining and implementing resources and capabilities in order to produce an outcome and *provide value* to customers or stakeholders.
	Processes are *strategic assets* when they create competitive advantage

and market differentiation. They *may* define roles, responsibilities, tools, management controls, policies, standards, guidelines, activities and work instructions if they are needed.

Service:
A means of delivering value to Customers by facilitating outcomes customers want to achieve without the ownership of specific costs or risks. The role of the Service Provider is to manage these costs and risks appropriately, spreading them over multiple customers if possible.

Functions:
A team or group of *people* and the tools they use to carry out one or more Processes or Activities. Functions provide units of organization responsible for specific outcomes. *ITIL® Functions covered include:*
- Service Desk
- Technical Management
- Application Management
- IT Operations Management.

Process Owner:
The person/role responsible for ensuring that the process is fit for the desired purpose and is accountable for the outputs of that process.
Example: The owner for the Availability Management Process

Service Owner:
The person/role accountable for the delivery of a specific IT Service. They are responsible for continual improvement and management of change affecting Services under their care.
Example: The owner of the Payroll Service

Process Manager:
The person/role responsible for the operational management of a process. There may be several managers for the one process. They report to the Process Owner.

Internal Service Providers:
An internal service provider that is embedded within a business unit e.g. one IT organization within each of the business units. The key factor is

that the *IT Services provide a source of competitive advantage* in the market space the business exists in.

Shared Service Providers:

An internal service provider that provides shared IT service to more than one business unit e.g. one IT organization to service all businesses in an umbrella organization. IT Services for this provider don't normally provide a source of competitive advantage, but instead *support effective and efficient business processes* across an organization.

External Service Providers:

Service provider that provides IT services to external customers. E.g. Providing internet hosting solutions for multiple customers.

Business Case:

A decision support and planning tool that projects the likely consequences of a business action. It provides justification for a significant item of expenditure. Includes information about costs, benefits, options, issues, risks and possible problems.

2.1 What are Services?

The concept of *IT Services* as opposed to *IT components* is central to understanding the Service Lifecycle and IT Service Management principles in general. It requires not just a learned set of skills, but also a way of thinking that often challenges the traditional instincts of IT workers to focus on the individual components (typically the applications or hardware under their care) that make up the IT infrastructure. The mindset requires instead an alternative outlook to be maintained, incorporating the 'end-to-end Service' perspective for what their organization actually provides to its customers.

The official definition of a Service is "a means of delivering value to customers by facilitating outcomes customers want to achieve without the ownership of specific costs or risks". Well what does this actually mean? To explain some of the key concepts I will use an analogy that most (food lovers) will understand.

While I do enjoy cooking, there are often times where I wish to enjoy quality food without the time and effort required to prepare a meal. If I was to cook, I would need to go to a grocery store, buy the ingredients, take these ingredients home, prepare and cook the meal, set the table and of course clean up the kitchen afterwards. The alternative, I can go to a restaurant that delivers a *service* that provides me with the same outcome (a nice meal) without the time, effort and general fuss required if I was to cook it myself.

Now consider how I would identify the quality and value of that service being provided. It isn't just the quality of the food itself that will influence my perceptions, but also:

- The cleanliness of the restaurant
- The friendliness and customer service skills of the waiters and other staff
- The ambience of the restaurant (lighting, music, decorations etc.)
- The time taken to receive my meal (and was it what I asked for?)
- Did they offer a choice of beverages?

If any one of these factors don't meet my expectations, then ultimately the perceived quality and value delivered to me as a customer is negatively impacted. Now, relate this to our role in provisioning an IT Service. If we, as IT staff, focus only on the application or hardware elements provided and forget or ignore the importance of the surrounding elements that make up the end-to-end service, just like in the example of the restaurant, the customer experience and perceived quality and value will be negatively impacted.

But if we take a Service-oriented perspective, we also ensure that:

- Communication with customers and end users is effectively maintained
- Appropriate resolution times are maintained for end user and customer enquiries
- Transparency and visibility of the IT organization and where money is being spent is maintained
- The IT organization works proactively to identify potential problems that should be rectified or improvement actions that could be made.

Using these principles, every phone call to the Service Desk or email request for a password reset, presents an opportunity to demonstrate service excellence and a commitment to our customers.

2.2 Processes & Functions

2.2.1 Defining Processes

Processes can be defined as a structured set of coordinated activities designed to produce an outcome and provide value to customers or stakeholders. A process takes one or more inputs, and through the activities performed, turns them into defined outputs.

Some principles:
- All processes should be measurable and performance-driven (not just in regards to time taken, but measuring overall efficiency including cost, effort and other resources used)
- All processes produce specific results that create value

- Processes are *strategic assets* when they create competitive advantage and market differentiation
- Processes *may* define roles, responsibilities, tools, management controls, policies, standards, guidelines, activities and work instructions if they are needed.

A *process owner* is the person responsible for ensuring that the process is fit for the desired purpose and is accountable for the outputs of that process.

A *process manager* is the person responsible for the operational management of a process. There may be several managers for the one process or the same person may be both the process owner and process manager (typically in smaller organizations).

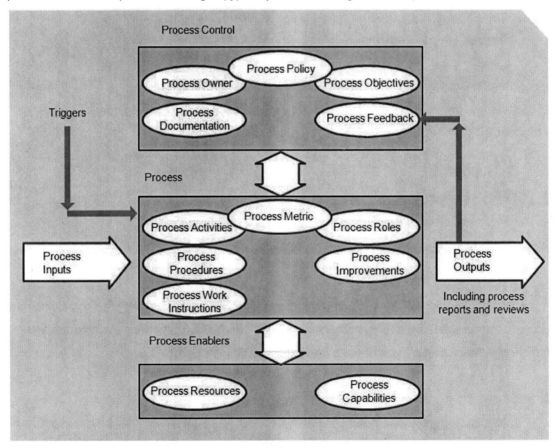

Figure 2.B – Generic Process Elements

The previous figure describes the physical components of processes, which are tangible and therefore typically get the most attention. In addition to the physical components, there are behavioral components which are for the most part intangible, and are part of an underlying pattern so deeply embedded and recurrent that it is displayed by most members of the organization and includes decision making, communication and learning processes. Behavioral components have no independent existence apart from the work processes in which they appear, but at the same time they greatly affect and impact the form, substance and character of activities and subsequent outputs by shaping how they are carried out.

So when defining and designing processes, it is important to consider both the physical and behavioral aspects that exist. This may be addressed by ensuring the all required stakeholders (e.g. staff members, customers and users etc.) are appropriately involved in the design of processes so that:

- They can communicate their own ideas, concerns and opinions that might influence the way in which processes are designed, implemented and improved. Of particular importance may be current behaviors that have not been previously identified which may affect the process design and implementation.
- Stakeholder groups are provided adequate training and education regarding how to perform their role within the process and what value the process provides for.
- Stakeholders generally feel to be empowered in the change being developed, and therefore are more likely to respond positively rather than actively or passively resisting the organizational changes occurring.

2.2.2 Defining Functions

Functions refer to the logical grouping of roles and automated measures that execute a defined process, an activity or combination of both. The functions that will be discussed within the Service Operation phase are needed to manage the 'steady state' operation IT environment. Just like in many sporting activities where each player will have a specific role to play in the overall team strategy, IT Functions define the different roles and responsibilities required for the overall design, delivery and management IT Services.

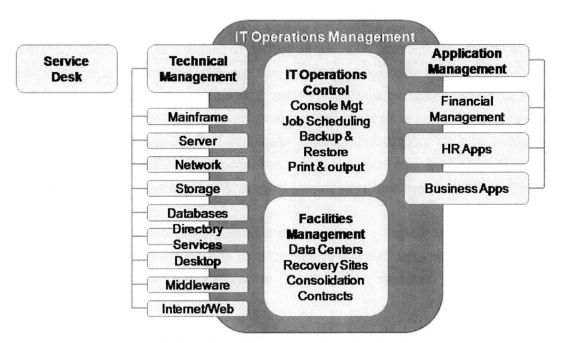

Figure 2.C – The ITIL® Functions from Service Operation

2.2.3 RACI Model

It is said that processes are perfect...until people get involved. This saying comes from the perceived failure of processes in many organizations, which can frequently be attributed to misunderstandings of the people involved and a lack of clarity regarding the roles and responsibilities that exist.

A useful tool to address this issue, assisting the definition of the roles and responsibilities when designing processes, is the RACI Model. RACI stands for:

R – Responsibility (actually does the work for that activity but reports to the function or position that has an "A" against it.)

A – Accountability (is made accountable for ensuring that the action takes place, even if they might not do it themselves. This role implies ownership.)

C – Consult (advice/ guidance/ information can be gained from this function or position prior to the action taking place.)

I – Inform (the function or position that is told about the event after it has happened.)

	Service Desk	Desktop	Applications	Operations Manager
Logging	RACI			CI
Classification	RACI	RCI		CI
Investigation	ACI	RCI	RCI	CI

Figure 2.D – The RACI Model

A RACI Model is used to define the roles and responsibilities of various Functions in relation to the activities of Incident Management.

General Rules that exist:

- Only 1 "A" per row can be defined (ensures accountability, more than one "A" would confuse this).
- At least 1 "R" per row must be (shows that actions are taking place), with more than one being appropriate where there is shared responsibility.

In the example RACI model given, the Service Desk is both responsible and accountable for ensuring that incidents are logged and classified, but not responsible for the subsequent investigation, which in this case will be performed by other functional teams.

3 The Service Lifecycle

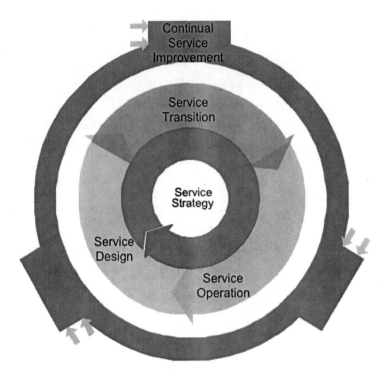

Figure 3.A – ITIL® Service Lifecycle Model

© Crown Copyright 2007 Reproduced under license from OGC

Lifecycle: The natural process of stages that an organism or inanimate object goes through as it matures. For example, human stages are birth, infant, toddler, child, pre-teen, teenager, young adult, adult, elderly adult and death.

The concept of the *Service Lifecycle* is fundamental to ITIL® Version 3. Previously, much of the focus of ITIL® was on the *processes* required to design, deliver and support services for customers. As a result of this previous focus on processes, Version 2 of the ITIL® Framework provided best practices for ITSM based around the *how* questions. These included:

- How should we design for availability, capacity and continuity of services?
- How can we respond to and manage incidents, problems and known errors?

As Version 3 now maintains a holistic view covering the entire lifecycle of a service, no longer does ITIL® just answer the how questions, but also *why?*

- Why does a customer need this service?
- Why should the customer purchase services from us?
- Why should we provide (x) levels of availability, capacity and continuity?

By first asking these questions it enables a service provider to provide overall *strategic objectives* for the IT organization, which will then be used to direct *how* services are *designed, transitioned, supported and improved* in order to deliver optimum value to customers and stakeholders.

The ultimate success of service management is indicated by the strength of the relationship between customers and service providers. The 5 phases of the Service Lifecycle provide the necessary guidance to achieve this success. Together they provide a body of knowledge and set of good practices for successful service management.

This end-to-end view of how IT should be integrated with business strategy is at the heart of ITIL's® five core volumes.

3.1 Mapping the Concepts of ITIL® to the Service Lifecycle

There has been much debate as to exactly how many processes exist within Version 3 of ITIL®. Questions asked include:

- What exactly constitutes a process?
- Shouldn't some processes be defined as functions?
- Why has x process been left out?

In developing this material, we have based our definitions of processes and functions and where they fit on the guidance provided by the ITIL® Foundation syllabus by EXIN International. Figure 3.B demonstrates the processes and functions of ITIL® in relation to the 5 Service Lifecycle Phases. It also demonstrates the increased scope now covered by ITIL® Version 3.

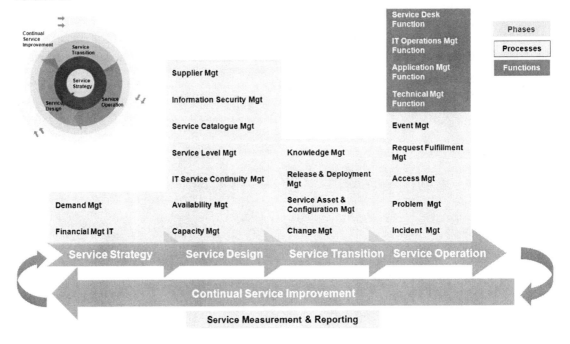

Figure 3.B – The Major Concepts of ITIL®

Note:

- The Service Lifecycle phases (and ITIL® books) are shown through the arrows at the bottom
- The concepts in light shading are the ITIL® V3 processes covered within the program
- The concepts in dark shading are Functions
- Processes that are not covered by the current ITIL V3 Foundation syllabus (currently 4.2), are not discussed fully in this book, but will be referenced where necessary for understanding.

3.2 How does the Service Lifecycle work?

Although there are five phases throughout the Lifecycle, they are not separate, nor are the phases necessarily carried out in a particular order. The whole ethos of the Service Lifecycle approach is that each phase will affect the other, creating a continuous cycle. For this to work successfully, the Continuous Service Improvement (CSI) phase is incorporated throughout all of the other phases. Figure 3.C demonstrates some of the key outputs from each of the Service Lifecycle Phases.

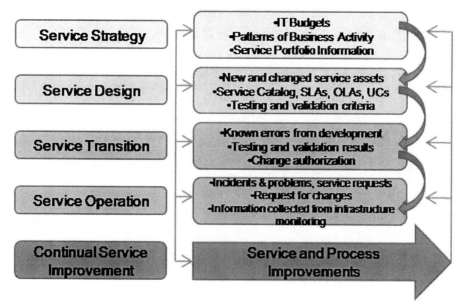

Figure 3.C – How does the Service Lifecycle Work?

It is important to note that most of the processes defined do not get executed within only one lifecycle phase.

Service Strategy Phase: Determine the needs, priorities, demands and relative importance for desired services. Identifies the value being created through services and the predicted financial resources required to design, deliver and support them.

Service Design Phase: Designs the infrastructure, processes and support mechanisms needed to meet the Availability requirements of the customer.

Service Transition Phase: Validates that the Service meets the functional and technical fitness criteria to justify release to the customer.

Service Operation Phase: Monitors the ongoing Availability being provided. During this phase we also manage and resolve incidents that affect Service Availability.

Continual Service Improvement Phase: Coordinates the collection of data, information and knowledge regarding the quality and performance of services supplied and Service Management activities performed. Service Improvement Plans developed and coordinated to improve any aspect involved in the management of IT services.

4 Service Strategy

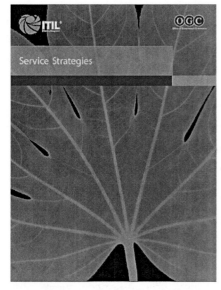

Figure 4.A: Service Strategy

The Service Strategy phase is concerned predominantly with the development of capabilities for Service Management, enabling these practices (along with the IT organization in general) to become a strategic asset of the organization. The guidance provided by the volume can be summarized as:

- Understanding the principles of Service Strategy.
- Developing Service Strategy within Service Management.
- Developing strategies for services and services for strategies.
- How strategy affects the Service Lifecycle.
- Strategies for organizational and cultural change.

4.1 Objectives of Service Strategy

The primary objectives of Service Strategy are to:

- Design, develop and implement service management as a strategic asset and to assist growth of the organization
- Develop the IT organization's capability to manage the costs and risks associated with their service portfolios
- Define, review and update the strategic objectives of the IT organization.

By achieving these objectives it will ensure that the IT organization has a clear understanding of how it can better support business growth, efficiency improvements or other strategies that wish to be realized.

KEY ROLE: To stop and think about WHY something has to be done, before thinking HOW.

4.2 Benefits of Service Strategy

Service Strategy has the potential for many significant benefits to be delivered to the IT organization and the business/customers it serves. However in many cases, these benefits fail to be realized due to insufficient connection and interfaces with other elements of the Service Lifecycle. For example:

The IT Strategy Group from an international banking and managed investment firm has decided to address the current economic downturn by reducing investments into the IT organization and Service Portfolio. As a result, the quality of some key services fall, with the support organization struggling to respond effectively to all calls for assistance. After a few months of lowered quality of service, the organization loses a number of major customers to their primary competitors. In response to the loss of these customers, further budget reductions are planned to counter the decrease in revenue earned.

By failing to realize their customers' value perception of services through service quality, the organization became caught in a negative cycle with potentially serious long term consequences. The missing link between the decisions being made by the strategy group and the potential impact they may have on elements of service quality (in particular the support of services in this example) or service value is often a challenge when developing Service Strategy.

When developed successfully as part of a holistic IT Service Management implementation, effective Service Strategy can provide:

- Improved understanding of the IT organization's customers and market space they reside in
- Detection and analysis of patterns in the demand for and use of IT services
- Improved understanding of the costs involved in providing and supporting IT services
- Identification and communication of the business value provided by IT services
- Enhanced capabilities for managing the overall portfolio of services, and in particular, optimizing investments into IT
- Consistent policies, standards and guidelines by which IT Service Management processes can align to.

4.3 Major Concepts

4.3.1 Creating Service Value

Perhaps historically, both providers and customers have used price as the focal point for communication and negotiation, but it is this path that ultimately leads to a negative experience for both parties. One of the key mantras that exist for any modern Service provider (IT or otherwise) is that it is essential to clearly establish value before you can attach a price to the services offered. This ensures a few key things:

- It avoids an apple to oranges comparison, which usually occurs with a price focal point
- It enables the Service Provider to distinguish their capabilities and differentiation from their competitors
- It clearly communicates to the customer what they can expect to receive as part of the delivery service.

Providers of IT Services need to take special appreciation of the concept of value creation and communication, due to the many misunderstandings about technology on behalf of customers (and poor communication by their IT providers). To address this issue, a central theme throughout the Service Strategy is value creation through services.

To explain the concept of value creation, the example of an Internet Service Provider (ISP) will be used throughout the next few sections.

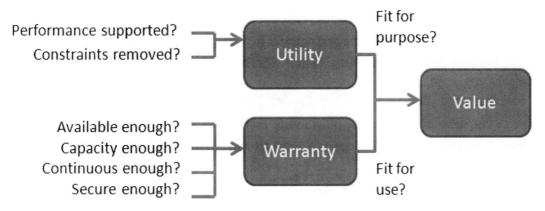

Figure 4.B – Creating Service Value

© Crown Copyright 2007 Reproduced under license from OGC

Important Formula: Service Warranty + Service Utility = Service Value

Service Utility describes the positive effect on business processes, activities, objects and tasks. This could be the removal of constraints that improves performance or some other positive effect that improves the outcomes managed and focused on by the customer and business. This is generally summarized as being fit for purpose.

In the case of a service provided by an ISP, examples of Service Utility could be:

- Ability to shop and bank online
- Communicate easily with friends and family around the world, without incurring an expensive phone bill
- Remove the need to always be 'at the office', instead allowing an individual to work or run their business from home.

Service Warranty on the other hand describes how well these benefits are delivered to the customer. It describes the Service's attributes such as the availability, capacity, performance, security and continuity levels to be delivered by the provider. Importantly, the Service Utility potential is only realized when the Service is available with sufficient capacity and performance.

Examples of Service Warranty for the previously mentioned ISP are:

- The connection speed of the internet service
- The download quota provided (20 GBs per month)
- The coverage of the service and network (e.g. for mobile broadband)
- The availability of support (e.g. 6am – 10pm).

By describing both *Service Utility* and *Service Warranty*, it enables the provider to clearly establish the value of the Service, differentiate themselves from the competition and, where necessary, attach a meaningful price tag that has relevance to the customer and associated market space.

4.3.2 Service Packages and Service Level Packages

Some customers have high utility requirements, some have high warranty requirements, and some require high levels of both. To accommodate this, Service Providers can seek to satisfy one or more of these types of customers by packaging different levels of Service Utility and Service Warranty, and pricing these packages accordingly.

To discuss Service Packages, Service Level Packages and how they are used to offer choice and value to customers, we're going to use the example of the packages made available by typical Internet Service Providers (ISPs).

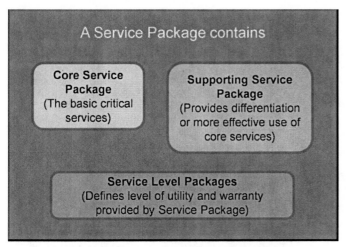

Figure 4.C – Service Package Example

A **Service Package** provides a detailed description of package of bundled services available to be delivered to customers. The contents of a Service Package includes:

- The core services provided
- Any supporting services provided
- The Service Level Package.

Figure 4.D – Service Level Package Example

Service Level Packages are effective in developing service packages with levels of utility and warranty appropriate to the customer's needs and in a cost-effective way.

- Availability and Capacity Levels
- Continuity Measures
- Security Levels
- Support arrangements (e.g. hours of support).

As customers, we have a wide range of choice when looking for an ISP to provide broadband internet. As a result, ISPs need to work hard to attract customers by communicating the value that they provide through their offerings. They also need to offer a wide range of choice for customers, who have varying requirements and needs for their broadband internet service.

So for our ISP example, we can define a Service Package in the following way:

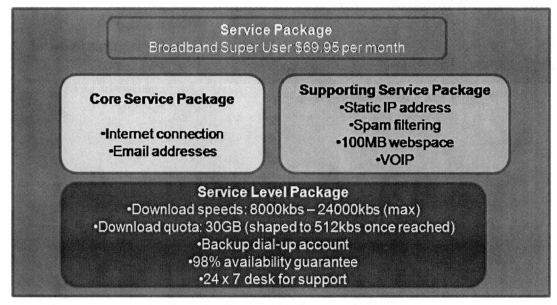

Figure 4.E – Detailed Service Package Example (ISP)

Most of the components of Service Packages and Service Level Packages are reusable components of the IT organization (many of which are services). Other components include software, hardware and other infrastructure elements. By providing Service Level Packages in this way it reduces the cost and complexity of providing services while maintaining high levels of customer satisfaction. In our example above, the ISP can easily create multiple Service Packages with varying levels of Utility and Warranty provided in order to offer a wide range of choice to customers, and to distinguish themselves from their competition.

The use of Service Packages and Service Level Packages enables Service Providers to avoid a one-size fits all approach to IT Services, while still maintaining efficiency of operations.

4.3.3 Service Assets

A Service Asset is any resource or capability used in the provision of services. Organizations use them to **create value** in the form of goods and services for customers.

Resources	Capabilities
Input to a process is consumed and manipulated to produce an output.	Used to coordinate, control and deploy resources.
Easy to acquire, can typically purchase or procure.	Experience-driven, information-based, needs to develop and mature over time.
Tangible, often a physical product.	Intangible, often made up of behaviors and experience that has developed over time.
Examples: IT Infrastructure, people or money	Examples: Teams, processes, behaviors, knowledge.

So while it is relatively easy for an organization to increase the capacity of its infrastructure, it is far more difficult and complex to improve the organization's capabilities for managing capacity and performance in a cost-effective manner. Service Strategy should seek to optimize the use and implementation of Service Assets, according to the needs and objectives of the business.

4.3.4 Risk

Risk is defined as uncertainty of outcome, whether it may result in a positive opportunity or negative threat. Managing risks requires the identification and control of the exposure to risk, which if materialized may have an impact on the achievement of an organization's business objectives. Every organization manages its risk, but not always in a way that is visible, repeatable and consistently applied to support decision making.

This is true for many organizations, where one of the greatest risk factors is a lack of accurate information when making decisions. The goal of risk management is to ensure that the organization makes cost-effective use of a risk framework that has a series of well-defined steps. The aim is to support better decision making, through a good understanding of risks and their likely impact.

Service Strategy should seek to maintain the appropriate balance of risk and reward in regards to investments and capabilities invested and maintained for IT.

4.3.5 The Service Portfolio

A Service Portfolio describes a provider's services in terms of business value. It includes the complete set of services managed by a Service Provider, providing a means for comparing service value across multiple providers. The portfolio is used to articulate business needs and the Service Provider's response to those needs. It is possible for a Service Provider to have multiple Service Portfolios depending on the customer groups that they support. The information contained within the portfolio is used to manage the entire lifecycle of all services, for one or more customers.

Services are grouped into three distinct categories in the Service Portfolio:

- Service Pipeline (services that have been proposed or are in development)
- Service Catalog (live services or those available for deployment)
- Retired Services (decommissioned services).

The information making up the Service Portfolio(s) will come from many sources, so possible implementations may make use of existing databases and other data repositories, document management systems, financial systems, project management documentation, the Service Catalog and other relevant input areas. Where necessary, the various sources of information may be collated and communicated by means of an internet/intranet-based interface, so that duplication does not occur and that appropriate levels of detail and accessibility can be controlled.

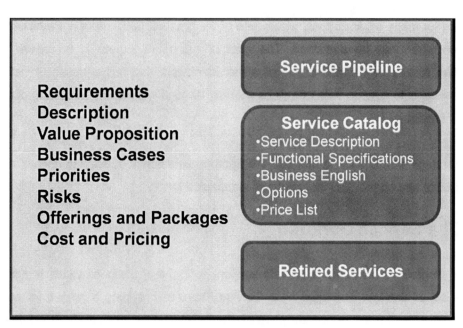

Figure 4.F – A Service Portfolio

By delivering the objectives above, the Service Portfolio either answers or helps to answer the following strategic questions:

- Why should a customer buy these services?
- Why should they buy these services from us?
- What are the pricing or chargeback models?
- What are our strengths and weaknesses, priorities and risks?
- How are resources and capabilities to be allocated?

Understanding their options helps senior executives to make informed investment decisions in service initiatives, taking into account appropriate levels of risks and rewards. These initiatives may cross business functions and may span short, medium and longer time frames.

Investment categories & Budget Allocations

Service Investments are split among 3 strategic categories:

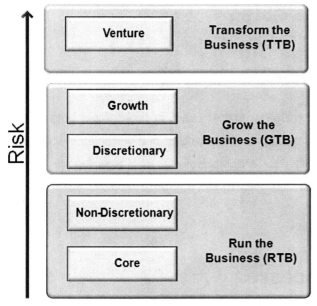

Figure 4.G – Balancing a Service Portfolio

© *Crown Copyright 2007 Reproduced under license from OGC*

Transform the Business (TTB):

TTB investments are focused on initiatives that enter new market spaces with new capabilities being developed.

Grow the business (GTB):

GTB investments are intended to grow the organization's scope of services, or gain more customers within an existing market space.

Run the business (RTB):

RTB investments are centered on maintaining service operations.

Service Retirement

An often over- looked investment, this is potentially one of the largest hidden costs in a service provider's organization, particularly in a large organization with a long history. Few providers have a clear plan for retiring increasingly redundant services. This is often due to a number of reasons, including a lack of visibility of what services are actually offered, and the fear that retiring a service may impact other services being offered.

Refreshing the Portfolio

The methods used by the Service Portfolio Manager and other involved stakeholders seek to continually refresh the Service Portfolio, creating service investments that provide an optimum balance of risk and reward.

Changes occur to the conditions within every market space, invalidating previous Return on Investment (ROI) calculations. Some of these changes may be a result of:

- New competitors or alternative options entering a market
- The introduction of new compliance regulations
- Mergers and acquisitions
- New or changed public legislation
- Changes in the economic climate affecting various markets.

The role of the Chief Information Officer (or other similar roles) in this context is to monitor, measure, reassess and rebalance investments as the markets and associated businesses change. They will need to identify what balance is appropriate for their organization (e.g. low risk and low reward, high risk and potential high reward) and authorize service investments that match these needs.

4.4 Service Strategy Processes

The processes included in the Service Strategy lifecycle phase are:

- Financial Management
- Demand Management.

These two processes work together to enable an IT organization to maximize the value of services being provided to customers and supply quality information to other ITSM processes. Although they are primarily strategic in nature, these processes also incorporate activities that are performed through all phases of the Service Lifecycle.

4.4.1 Financial Management

GOAL: The goal of Financial Management is to provide cost effective stewardship of the IT assets and the financial resources used in providing IT services. Primarily this is to enable an organization to account fully for the financial resources consumed by the IT service provider and to attribute these costs to the services delivered to the organization's customers.

Financial Management is focused on providing both the business and IT with improved insight (in financial terms) into the value of IT services, supporting assets and operational management and support. This translates into improved operational visibility, insight and superior decision-making at all levels of the organization.

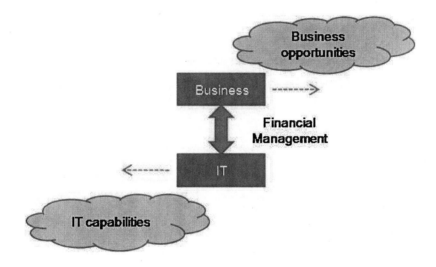

Figure 4.H – Financial Management managing conflicting perspectives

When implemented effectively, Financial Management provides the understanding and management of the distance and (sometimes) conflicting perspectives between the Business Desires/Opportunities and the Capabilities of the IT organization. It enables the business to be more IT conscious and IT to become more business-aligned.

As businesses evolve, markets change and the IT industry matures, Financial Management is becoming increasingly adopted by IT organizations, with typical benefits including:

- Enhanced decision making
- Increased speed of change
- Improved Service Portfolio Management
- Financial compliance and control
- Improved operational control
- Greater insight and communication of the value created by IT services.

4.4.1.1 Activities

There are three fundamental activities for Financial Management for IT Services. These are:

- Funding
- IT Accounting
- Chargeback.

Funding: Predicting the expected future requirements for funds to deliver the agreed upon services and monitoring adherence to the defined budgets. This ensures that the required resources to fund IT are made available and can improve the business case for IT projects and initiatives.

IT Accounting: Enables the IT organization to account fully for the way its money is spent. The definition of Cost Models can be used to identify costs by customer, by service, by activity or other logical groupings. IT Accounting supports more accurate budgeting and ensures that any charging method utilized is simple, fair and realistic.

Chargeback: Charging customers for their use of IT Services. Charging can be implemented in a number of ways in order to encourage more efficient use of IT resources. Notional charging is one particular option, in which the costs of providing Services to customers are communicated but no actual payment is required.

4.4.1.2 Other Terminology

Terminology	Explanations
Cost Types:	These are higher level expenses identified such as hardware, software, people, accommodation, transfer and external costs.
Cost Elements:	The actual elements making up the cost types above e.g. for the hardware cost type it would include the elements such as CPUs, Servers, Desktops etc.
Direct Costs:	Cost elements identified to be clearly attributed to only a single customer or service.
Indirect Costs:	Often known as overheads, these are costs that are shared across multiple customers or services, which have to be shared in a fair manner.
Cost Units:	A cost unit is the identified unit of consumption that is accounted for a particular service or service asset.

Financial Management assists in the role of Service Valuation, which is used to help the business and the IT Service Provider agree on the value of the IT Service. It determines the balance demonstrating the total cost of providing an IT Service against the total value offered to the business by the Service. As previously described in chapter 4.2, value in services is created by the combination of Service Utility and Service Warranty.

Demand Modeling:

Financial Management works closely with the process of Demand Management *(see chapter 4.3.3)* to anticipate usage of services by the business and the associated financial implications of future service demand. This assists in identifying the funding requirements for services, as well as input into proposed pricing models, including any incentives and penalties used.

Strategically, financial input can be gained from key times such as product launches, entry into new markets, mergers and acquisitions, which all generate specific patterns of demand. From a customer perspective, the Service Catalog should provide the capability to regulate their demands for IT services and prepare budgets, avoiding the problem of over-consumption.

4.4.2 Demand Management

Demand Management was previously an activity found within Capacity Management, and now within Version 3 of ITIL® it has been made a separate process found within the Service Strategy phase. The reasoning behind this is that before we decide how to design for capacity, decisions must be made regarding why demand should be managed in a particular way. Such questions asked here include:

- When and why does the business need this capacity?
- Does the benefit of providing the required capacity outweigh the costs?
- Why should the demand for services be managed to align with the IT strategic objectives?

Poorly managed demand is a particular source of risk for service providers, with potential negative impacts being felt by both the IT organizations and customers. If demand is not accurately predicted and managed, idle (excess) capacity will generate cost without creating associated value that can be appropriately recovered. From the customer perspective, most would be highly reluctant to pay for idle capacity unless it provides some value for them.

On the other hand, insufficient capacity can impact the quality of services delivered, potentially limiting the growth desired for services and for the organization as a whole. Accordingly, Demand Management must seek to achieve a balance between the prediction and management of demand for services against the supply and production of capacity to meet those demands. By doing so, both the customers and IT can reduce excess capacity needs while still supporting required levels of quality and warranty in agreed services.

Keep in mind that Demand Management plays an integral part in supporting the objectives of an organization and maximizing the value of the IT Service Provider. This means that the way in which Demand Management is utilized will vary greatly between each organization. Two examples showing these differences are:

Health Organizations: When providing IT Services that support critical services being offered to the public, it would be unlikely that there would be many (if any) Demand Management restrictions that would be utilized, as the impact of these restrictions could lead to tragic implications for patients being treated.

Commercial Confectionery Organizations: Typically a confectionery company will have extremely busy periods around traditional holidays (e.g. Christmas). Demand Management techniques would be utilized to promote more cost-effective use of IT during the non-peak periods; however leading up to these holidays the service provider would seek to provide all capacity to meet demand and support higher revenue streams for the business units involved.

4.4.2.1 Goal and objectives

The primary goal of Demand Management is to assist the IT Service Provider in understanding and influencing *customer demand* for services and the provision of *Capacity* to meet these demands.

Other objectives include:

- Identification and analysis of Patterns of Business Activity (PBA) and user profiles that generate demand
- Utilizing techniques to influence and manage demand in such a way that excess capacity is reduced but the business and customer requirements are still satisfied.

4.4.2.2 Activity-based Demand Management

The primary source of demand for IT services comes from the execution of business process within the organization(s) being served. With any business process, there will be a number of variations in workload that will occur, which are identified as patterns of business activity (PBA) so that their affect on demand patterns can be understood. By understanding exactly how the customer's business activity operates, the IT organization can improve the way in which capacity is planned and produced for any supporting services.

Demand occurs at multiple levels. Increased workload in the business can translate to a higher utilization of services by existing employees. At the same time, additional staff members that are employed by the organization can be translated into additional demands to the IT service provider (especially the Service Desk) in terms of service requests and incidents. To manage this, regular communication is required so that the business plans of the customers and business units are synchronized with the service management plans of the service provider.

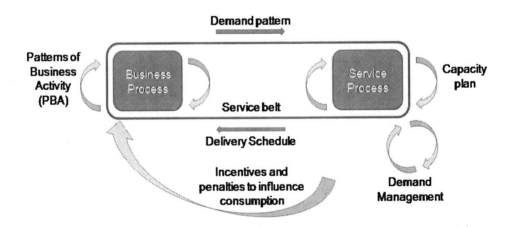

Figure 4.1: – Activity-based Demand Management
© Crown Copyright 2007 Reproduced under license from OGC

Over time, Demand Management should be able to build a profile of business processes and patterns of business activity in such a way that seasonal variations as well as specific events (e.g. adding new employees) can be anticipated in terms of associated demand. Using this information will help various elements of the Service Lifecycle, including the following:

Service Design: Particularly Capacity and Availability Management, which can optimize designs to suit demand patterns.

Service Transition: Change Management and Service Validation and Testing can ensure that appropriate levels of warranty can be provided.

Service Operation: Can optimize the availability of staff based on patterns of demand.

Continual Service Improvement: Can identify opportunities to consolidate demand or introduce improved incentives or techniques to be utilized in influencing demand.

Critical to the effective application of Demand Management is a forward-looking Capacity Plan, which should identify how capacity will be produced to meet the predicted demand patterns, including the level of excess capacity deemed appropriate in accordance with the business requirements for service value.

4.4.2.3 User Profiles

Like patterns of business activity (PBA), User profiles should be identified and analyzed for their relationship to the patterns of demand generated in the business. User profiles are defined in the context of the roles and responsibilities within the organization for people, functions, processes and applications. In some cases a user profile will be defined for an automated process, which will have its own demand for supporting services.

When defining user profiles, they will be associated with one or more PBA, which requires both customers and the service provider to have a clear understanding of the business activities and how various roles are related.

The following table is an example of User profiles defined by Demand Management:

User profile	Applicable pattern of business activity	PBA code
Senior Executive (UP 1)	Moderate domestic and international travel, highly sensitive information to be protected, high urgency for service requests, communication services need to be highly available.	33B 17D 21A
Office-based managers	Low domestic and international travel, medium sensitive information, medium urgency for service requests, communication services need to be highly available.	33D 17B 21A
Office-based staff	No domestic and international travel, low sensitive information, low urgency for service requests, communication services require medium availability.	33A 17E 21C

In the table, the PBA code would be referencing previously defined patterns of business activity, which helps clarify when will each type of user typically generate demand for IT services and what level of demand will there be. This is valuable information which can be used for then predicting the potential impact that adding or removing staff members (users) may have on the demand for IT services, and the ability of the IT service provider to meet those demands.

4.4.2.4 Developing differentiated offerings

Demand Management needs to work closely with the other ITSM processes (Financial Management and Service Level Management) in ensuring the appropriate development of Services that suit identified patterns and types of demand. This may be as simple as Gold, Silver and Bronze offerings to influence the adoption and use of IT services. To clarify how Demand Management works with other ITSM processes, the following is a summary of the various actions performed:

Service Portfolio Management responsibilities – to assess, manage and prioritize investments into IT, identifying underserved, well-served and over-served demand. Manage Service Portfolio, including the definition of services in terms of business value.

Demand Management responsibilities – identify, develop and analyze PBA and user profiles. Build capabilities for predicting seasonal variations and specific events in terms of the associated demand generated. Strategically package services to reduce excess capacity needs while still meeting business requirements. Design and apply techniques where necessary to influence demand.

Financial Management responsibilities – to work with Demand Management to determine value of services (and understand the effect on value by varying levels of capacity and performance), and to develop appropriate chargeback models to be used in influencing demand.

Service Level Management responsibilities – to maintain regular communication with customers and business units, identify any potential issues, promote service catalog, negotiate and agree relevant SLAs (including the charging mechanisms used to influence demand), ensure correct alignment of Service Packages and Service Level Packages. Generally measure the success of IT and quality of service delivered from the customer perspective, providing feedback to the other processes on issues and potential improvements.

4.4.2.5 Influencing Demand

The two primary methods used to influence or manage demand:

- Physical/Technical constraints e.g. restrict number of connections, users, running times
- Financial chargeback e.g. using expensive charging for services near full capacity or over capacity quotas.

Example

Every morning between 8:00am and 8:30am, approximately 1500 users logon to the network. At the same time, many IT services, batch jobs and reports are run by various groups throughout the organization.

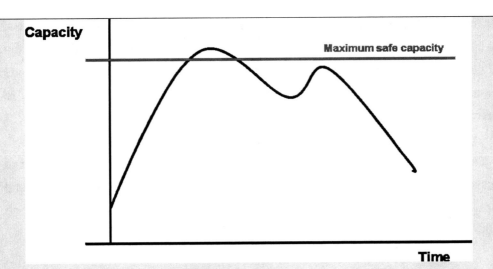

Figure 4.J – Using Demand Management to Optimize IT Capacity

Recently the performance of the IT infrastructure has been experiencing problems during this time period (e.g. taking a long time to log on, reports and batch jobs failing). Outside of this time, the IT infrastructure performs at acceptable levels.

What are some Demand Management techniques that could be utilized to address this situation?

Possible techniques:

- Staggering work start times for employees
- Prioritizing reports and batch jobs
- Running non-time-critical reports and batch jobs at night or outside typical work hours
- Restricting any non-critical activities during peak periods.

4.5 Service Strategy Summary

The Service Strategy phase enables the organization to ensure that the organizational objectives for IT are defined and that Services and Service Portfolios are maximized for value. Other benefits delivered include:

- Enhanced ability to predict the resources required to fund IT
- Clearer visibility of the costs for providing IT Services
- Quality information to support investment decisions in IT
- Understanding of the use and demand for IT Services, with the ability to influence positive and cost-effective use of IT.

As the focal point for strategy, policy and guidelines that direct the efforts and practices of the IT organization, Service Strategy has many important interfaces with the rest of the Service Lifecycle. Some of these include:

- Interfaces with the Service Design phase:
  o Service Archetypes and Models, which describe how service assets interact with customer assets. These are important high-level inputs that guide the design of services
  o Definition of business outcomes to be supported by services
  o Understanding of varying priority in required service attributes
  o Relative design constraints for the service (e.g. budget, contractual terms and conditions, copyrights, utility, warranty, resources, standards and regulations etc.)
  o Definition of the cost models associated with providing services.

- Interfaces with the Service Transition phase:
  o Service Transition provides evaluations of the costs and risks involved with introducing and modifying services. It also provides assistance in determining the relative options or paths for changing strategic positions or entering market spaces
  o Request for Changes may be utilized to affect changes to strategic positions
  o Planning of the required resources and evaluation whether the change can be implemented fast enough to support the strategy

- o Control and recording of service assets is maintained by Service Asset and Configuration Management.

- Interfaces with the Service Operation phase:
  - o Service Operation will deploy service assets in patterns that most effectively deliver the required utility and warranty in each segment across the Service Catalog.
  - o Deployment of shared assets that provide multiple levels of redundancy, support a defined level of warranty and build economies of scale.
  - o Service Strategy must clearly define the warranty factors that must be supported by Service Operation, with attributes of reliability, maintainability, redundancy and overall experience of availability.

- Interfaces with the Continual Service Improvement phase:
  - o Continual Service Improvement (CSI) will provide the coordination and analysis of the quality, performance and customer satisfaction of the IT organization, including the processes utilized and services provided.
  - o Integration with CSI will also provide the identification of potential improvement actions that can be made to elements of Service Strategy.

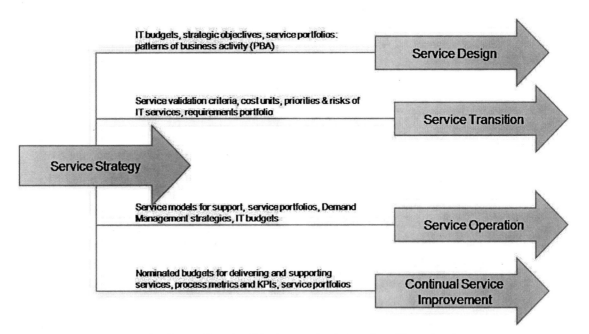

Figure 4.K – Some Service Strategy outputs to other lifecycle phases.

Service Strategy Service Scenario

To assist with your learning and understanding of how the phases and processes work together, the following scenario will be used throughout this book.

This simplistic overview of a service gives examples of how the processes are utilized to create the service.

The business has requested that they would like to be able to use the internet for instant messaging with international offices. They are also interested in VOIP and video conferencing. We shall call this new service HYPE. This scenario will continue throughout the rest of the book.

Overall Service Strategy

- It is important here to truly understand exactly what the business needs are, as well as their expectations for this service
- Value must be defined (remember that utility + warranty = value):
    - Utility considers the features of HYPE – what type of support will the business require, what features will the business want/need i.e. is it fit for purpose?
    - Warranty considers the levels of service guarantee (e.g. continuity, availability, security, capacity) that the business requires to be clarified – this is set out in service level packages
- Service Level Packages:
    - Core service package – instant messaging
    - Supporting service package – added VOIP and/or Video conferencing, ability to attach files
    - Service Level packages – video quality, security of transmissions, access times, service support, user access.

Service Portfolio Considerations

- You have already been trialing X brand instant messenger service among the IT staff, so an entry has been added to the Service Pipeline
- Are there redundant services to retire?

Financial Management Considerations

- Cost to purchase/build service
- Cost of hardware (web cams, PC upgrades if necessary)
- Cost of increased internet access/bandwidth
- Charging for service?
- Budget?

Demand Management Considerations

- When would business most need service? (Mornings and afternoons, as they are most likely to interact with international counterparts - time zones, times of year?)
- What measures can we take to manage demand?
- Limit VOIP/video to certain groups/users
- Charge business for use
- Dedicated bandwidth across whole of service.

By determining the above before you start to design the service, you are in a better position to ensure that HYPE will meet the customer needs (closed loop system). Remember, this is where value is agreed, and Service Operation is where value of HYPE is seen. As we all know, the level of value will more than likely be in direct correlation to the dollars the business is prepared to pay, and this is why it is important to clarify this now, before we start designing.

4.6 Service Strategy Review Questions

These questions also cover the Introduction and Common Terminology Chapters.

Question 1

Which ITIL® process is responsible for developing a charging system?

a) Availability Management
b) Capacity Management
c) Financial Management for IT Services
d) Service Level Management

Question 2

What is the RACI model used for?

a) Documenting the roles and relationships of stakeholders in a process or activity
b) Defining requirements for a new service or process
c) Analyzing the business impact of an incident
d) Creating a balanced scorecard showing the overall status of Service Management

Question 3

Which of the following identifies two Service Portfolio components within the Service Lifecycle?

a) Catalog Service Knowledge Management System and Requirements Portfolio
b) Service Catalog and Service Pipeline
c) Service Knowledge Management System and Service Catalog
d) Service Pipeline and Configuration Management System

Question 4

Which of the following is NOT one of the ITIL® core publications?

a) Service Operation
b) Service Transition
c) Service Derivation
d) Service Strategy

Question 5

A Service Level Package is best described as?

a) A description of customer requirements used to negotiate a Service Level Agreement
b) A defined level of utility and warranty associated with a core service package
c) A description of the value that the customer wants and for which they are willing to pay
d) A document showing the Service Levels achieved during an agreed reporting period

Question 6

Setting policies and objectives is the primary concern of which of the following elements of the Service Lifecycle?

a) Service Strategy
b) Service Strategy and Continual Service Improvement
c) Service Strategy, Service Transition and Service Operation
d) Service Strategy, Service Design, Service Transition, Service Operation and Continual Service Improvement

Question 7

A service owner is responsible for which of the following?

a) Designing and documenting a Service
b) Carrying out the Service Operations activities needed to support a Service
c) Producing a balanced scorecard showing the overall status of all Services
d) Recommending improvements

Question 8

The utility of a service is best described as:

a) Fit for design
b) Fit for purpose
c) Fit for function
d) Fit for use

Question 9

The 4 P's of ITSM are people, partners, processes and …?:

    a) Purpose
    b) Products
    c) Perspectives
    d) Practice

Question 10

The contents of a service package includes:

    a) Base Service Package, Supporting Service Package, Service Level Package
    b) Core Service Package, Supporting Process Package, Service Level Package
    c) Core Service Package, Base Service Package, Service Support Package
    d) Core Service Package, Supporting Services Package, Service Level Package

©The Art of Service

5 Service Design

Figure 5.A – Service Design

The Service Design phase is concerned predominantly with the design of IT Services, as well as the associated or required:

- Processes
- Service Management systems and tools
- Service Solutions
- Technology architectures
- Measurement systems.

The driving factor in the design of new or changed services is the support of changing business needs. Every time a new service solution is produced, it needs to be checked against the rest of the Service Portfolio to ensure that it will integrate and interface with all of the other services in existence.

5.1 Objectives

While there are many elements within the Service Design phase, the three main objectives that provide direction to the processes involved are:

- To convert the strategic objectives defined during Service Strategy into Services and Service Portfolios
- To use a holistic approach for design to ensure integrated end-to-end business related functionality and quality
- To ensure consistent design standards and conventions are followed in all services and processes being designed.

5.2 Major Concepts

An overall, integrated approach should be adopted for the design activities, covering five major aspects of Service Design:

1. **Service Portfolio:** Service Management systems and tools, especially the Service Portfolio for the management and control of services through their lifecycle.
2. **Service Solutions:** including documentation of all of the functional requirements, performance criteria, and other resources and capabilities needed and agreed.
3. **Technology architectures:** Technology architectures and management architectures and tools required to provide the service.
4. **Processes:** Processes needed to design, transition, operate and improve the service.
5. **Measurement systems:** Measurement systems, methods and metrics for the services, the architectures and their constituent components and the processes.

The key aspect in the design of new or changed services is to meet changing business needs. Every time a new service solution is produced, it needs to be checked against each of the other aspects to ensure that it will integrate and interface with all of the other services in existence.

5.2.1 Service Design Packages

The information contained within a Service Design Package includes documentation of all aspects of the service and its requirements, in order to provide guidance and structure through all of the subsequent stages of its lifecycle. The information contained within it should address the five major aspects of Service Design that were previously mentioned. A Service Design Package is typically produced for each new IT Service, major Change, or IT Service Retirement.

Service Design Packages	
• Business Requirements	• Organizational Readiness Assessment
• Service Applicability	• User Acceptance Test Criteria
• Service Contacts	• Service Program
• Service Functional Requirements	• Service Transition Plan
• Service Level Requirements	• Service Operational Plan
• Service Design and Topology	• Service Acceptance Criteria

5.3 Service Design Processes

The processes included with the Service Design lifecycle phase are:

- Service Level Management
- Capacity Management
- Availability Management
- IT Service Continuity Management
- Information Security Management
- Supplier Management
- Service Catalog Management.

It is important to note that many of the activities from these processes will occur in other lifecycle phases, especially Service Operation. Additionally, Service Level Management also plays an important role in Continual Service Improvement.

Like all ITIL processes, the level to which the Service Design processes are required to be implemented will depend on many factors, including:

- The complexity and culture of the organization
- The relative size, complexity and maturity of the IT infrastructure

- The type of business and associated customers being served by IT
- The number of services, customers and end users involved
- Regulations and compliance factors affecting the business or IT
- The use of outsourcing and external suppliers for small or large portions of the overall IT Service Delivery.

Based on these influencing factors, the SOA team may comprise of a single person in a small IT department, or a worldwide network of business and customer oriented groups in an international organization.

5.3.1 Service Level Management

5.3.1.1 Goal

The primary goal of Service Level Management is to ensure that an agreed level of IT service is provided for all current IT services, and that future services are delivered in line with agreed achievable targets. It also proactively seeks and implements improvements to the level of service delivered to customers and users.

While some organizations may continue to rely on a 'best endeavors' approach to service quality, the majority have realized that there needs to be a consistent, agreed and understandable method used for defining and reporting of IT service quality. As the modern IT organization has matured over time to be more akin to any other area of business, there has also been an increased requirement for more formal methods, by which the value of funding and investments into IT are assessed, and performance measured for services provided and capabilities supported. In the context of Service Offerings and Agreements, Service Level Management is the process that seeks to provide consistency in defining the requirements for services, documenting targets and responsibilities, and providing clarity as to the achievements for service quality delivered to customers.

In effect, the process seeks to manage the 'grey areas' that are formed between customers and the IT organization, as well as ensuring that the activities performed by various IT groups are coordinated optimally to meet customer requirements. The staff involved (Service Level Management team) are fluent in both technical and business jargon; they resolve disputes between parties (but as a result are sometimes seen as a spy in both camps) and generally work to improve the relationship between the IT organization and the customers it supports.

Terminology	Explanation
Service Level Agreement (SLA):	A written agreement between a service provider and their Customers that documents *agreed* levels of service for a Service.
Service Catalog:	A written statement of available IT services, default levels, options, prices and identification of which business processes or customers use them.
Underpinning Contract (UC):	Contract with an external supplier that supports the IT organization in their delivery of services.
Operational Level Agreement (OLA):	Internal agreement with another area of the same organization which supports the IT service provider in their delivery of services.
Service Level Requirements:	Detailed recording of the Customer's needs, forming the design criteria for a new or modified service.

5.3.1.2 Agreements and Contracts

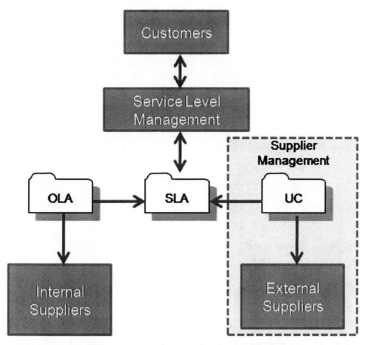

Figure 5.B – SLAs, OLAs and UCs

Negotiating and agreeing upon the SLAs and OLAs is the responsibility of Service Level Management. Supplier Management is responsible for negotiation and agreeing upon UCs with external suppliers. These two processes must communicate to ensure that the UCs do align with and support the SLAs in place.

What are the roles of OLAs and UCs?
They are agreements with other internal areas of the organization (e.g. the Service Desk, human resources) and external suppliers on how they support the IT organization in meeting the SLAs with customers.

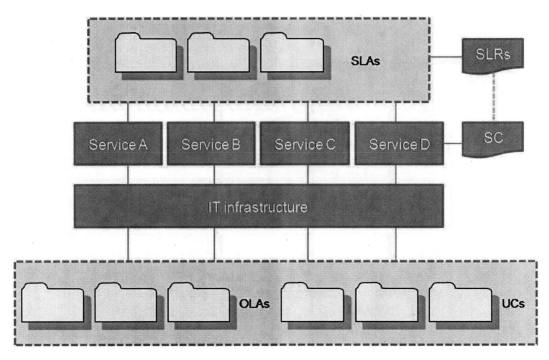

Figure 5.C – How SLAs, OLAs and UCs fit together

Question:

An organization is planning to formalize its IT Service Management practices, and wants to implement Service Level Management. At present, there is very little documentation of the services currently being provided to customers.

According to the ITIL® framework which of these documents should be developed first?

Answer: Normally the Service Catalog should be produced first because we need to define and agree what we actually are providing, and then we can map the customer requirements to the Service Catalog to see what gaps or redundant services exist. By rushing in to the creation of SLAs, it is likely they will develop into complex or inaccurate representations of service levels, and not help to manage the relationship between the service provider and customers.

Although Service Level Agreements are implemented in a wide variety of fashions, the guiding principle is that they are a written agreement between an IT service provider and the IT customer(s), defining the key service targets and responsibilities of both parties.

The key word here is agreement, in that SLAs should not be used as a way of holding one side or the other to ransom. When SLAs are viewed in a positive nature, a way of continually improving the relationship between provider and customers, mutually beneficial agreements will be developed. Viewing SLAs as just contracts can contribute to development of a 'blame culture' by both parties.

The level of technical detail included within the SLA will also vary, depending on the type and nature of the customer. Some customers may be an IT Service Provider themselves, others will be purely business focused. To be successful in all these scenarios, SLAs must be written in such a way that they are clear and unambiguous for both parties, leaving no room for confusion or misinterpretation. They certainly won't be perfect from the moment they are developed, so a continual cycle of review and revision should seek to improve the quality and effectiveness of SLAs over time.

5.3.1.3 Service Level Agreement Structures

There are a number of ways in which SLAs can be structured. The important factors to consider when choosing the SLA structure are:

- Will the SLA structure allow flexibility in the levels of service to be delivered for various customers?
- Will the SLA structure require much duplication of effort?
- Who will sign the SLAs?

Three types of SLAs structures that are discussed within ITIL® are service-based, customer-based and multi-level or hierarchical SLAs.

69   ©The Art of Service

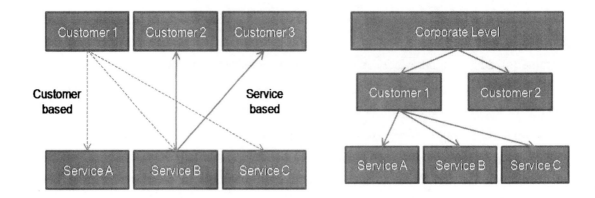

Figure 5.D – SLA structures

Many different factors will need to be considered when deciding which SLA structure is most appropriate for an organization to use.

Typical Multi-level SLA Structure components:

1. **Corporate level:** All generic issues are covered, which are the same for the entire organization.

   Example: *The Corporate Security Baseline, e.g. Passwords, ID cards etc.*

2. **Customer level:** Those issues specific to a customer can be dealt with.

   Example: *Security requirements of one or more departments within the organization are higher e.g. the financial department needs higher security measures.*

3. **Service Level:** All issues relevant to a specific service (in relation to customer) can be covered.

   Example: *The email services for a particular department needs encryption and secure backups.*

Using a multi-level structure for a large organization reduces the duplication of effort while still providing customization for customers and services (by inheritance).

5.3.1.4 The Typical Contents of SLAs

- An introduction to the SLA
- Service description
- Mutual responsibilities
- Scope of SLA
- Applicable service hours
- Service availability
- Reliability

- Customer support arrangements
- Contact points & escalation
- Service performance
- Batch turnaround times
- Security
- Costs and charging method used.

The key criteria for any information to be contained within an SLA is that it must be measureable, with all language used being clear and concise in order to aid understanding. As already discussed, SLAs should not only be used as legal documents for imposing penalties, otherwise it is in conflict with the goal of improving relationships between customers and the IT Service provider. Another mistake made by organizations in implementing SLAs is they that become too long and technically focused. When this occurs there is potential for misunderstandings or for the SLA to go unread.

5.3.1.5 Service Level Management Activities

As an overview of Service Level Management, the process will generally consist of the following interrelated activities: *(not necessarily in chronological order)*

1. Develop contacts and relationships
2. Design an SLA framework
3. Determine, document and agree requirements for new services
4. Negotiate and develop SLAs
5. Review and revise SLAs, underpinning agreements, Operational Level Agreements and service scope
6. Monitoring service performance against SLAs
7. Produce service reports
8. Conduct service reviews and instigate improvements within an overall Service Improvement Plan (SIP)
9. Collate measure and improve customer satisfaction

10. Managing complaints and compliments.

5.3.1.6 Service Improvement Plans

Service Improvement Plans are formal plans to implement improvements to a process or service. They are used to ensure that improvement actions are identified and carried out on a regular basis.

The identified improvements may come from:
- Breaches of Service Level Agreements
- Identification of user training and documentation issues
- Weak system testing
- Identified weak areas within internal and external support groups.

5.3.1.7 Roles and Responsibilities

Service Level Manager:
- Must be senior enough to represent organization; with *authority* to do what is necessary
- Manages Service Catalog, SLAs and OLAs and ensures alignment of Underpinning Contracts
- Identifies and manages improvements to services and processes
- Analyzes and reports on Service Level Achievements.

Skills: Relationship Management, patience, tolerance, resilience and an understanding of the customer's business and how IT contributes to the delivery of that product or service.

5.3.1.8 Challenges Affecting Service Level Management
- Monitoring of pre-SLA achievements, where to begin?
- Identifying targets that are achievable and reasonable
- Insufficient focus, resources and time
- Inadequate seniority of SLM staff

- Underpinning contracts ignored
- SLAs too long, written in technical jargon and not customer focused
- Improvement actions not adhered to.

5.3.1.9 Service Level Management Metrics

Statistics:

- Number/percentage of services covered by SLAs
- Number/percentage of SLAs supported by UCs and OLAs
- Number/percentage of service targets being met

Yes/Why Questions:

- Are service level achievements improving?
- Are customer perception statistics improving?
- Are IT costs for service provisions decreasing for services with stable (acceptable but not improving) Service Level Achievements?

Implementing effective and efficient Service Level Management should produce a "Yes" answer to each of the above questions.

If the answer is No:

If the answer is "No" to any of these questions, the very next question that should be asked is "Why?"

From this we can investigate where the process is deficient and begin a plan for improvement. Communicating this to the business also gives them a better understanding of the complexity of providing the services and more importantly allows the business to be actively involved with assessing the costs, risks and plausibility of what will be needed in order to bridge the gap.

5.3.2 Supplier Management

"No man is an island".

This phrase comes from a longer quotation by John Donne (1572-1631). The general meaning is that human beings do not thrive when isolated from others; we are all connected and therefore events and changes affecting one human being affects us all.

Although abstract, this concept provides an engaging way in which a service provider should approach the management of IT services. Like the original quote, *no service provider is an island*, so events and changes affecting their customers and suppliers will in turn have some consequence for them.

What does this mean for IT Service Management? Based on this principle, we need to ensure that we carefully evaluate, select, manage and review any suppliers who will be involved in some way in the delivery and support of IT services, and be sure to develop and foster the relationship in a mutually beneficial way. As many organizations have found out recently, the death of a supplier (caused by economic downturn) may mean their own future could be short lived.

5.3.2.1 Goal and Objectives

The primary goal of Supplier Management is to manage suppliers and the services they supply, to provide seamless quality of IT service to the business and ensure that value for money is obtained.

Other objectives include the application of capabilities to:

- Obtain value for money from supplier and contracts
- Ensure that underpinning contracts and agreements with suppliers are aligned to business needs
- Manage relationships with suppliers
- Negotiate and agree contracts with suppliers
- Manage supplier performance
- Maintain a supplier policy and a supporting Supplier and Contract Database (SCD).

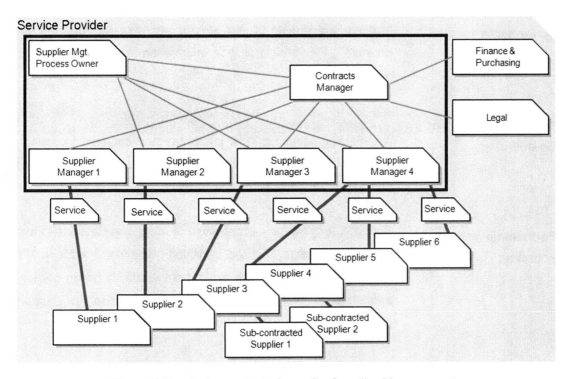

Figure 5.E: – Roles and interfaces for Supplier Management
© Crown Copyright 2007 Reproduced under license from OGC

Terminology	Explanation
Supplier service improvement plans (SSIP):	Used to record all improvement actions and plans agreed between suppliers and service providers.
Supplier Survey Reports:	Feedback gathered from all individuals that deal directly with suppliers throughout their day to day role. Results are collated and reviewed by Supplier Management, to ensure consistency in quality of service provided by suppliers in all areas.
Supplier & Contract performance reports:	Used as input for the Supplier & Contract review meetings to manage the quality of the service provided by suppliers and partners. This should include information on shared risk, when appropriate.

Types of Supplier Arrangements:

Co-sourcing:	An informal combination of insourcing and outsourcing, using a number of outsourcing organizations working together to co-source key elements within the lifecycle.
Partnership or multi-sourcing:	Formal arrangements between two or more organizations to work together to design, develop transition, maintain, operate, and/or support IT service(s). The focus here tends to be on strategic partnerships that leverage critical expertise or market opportunities.
Business Process Outsourcing:	Formal arrangements where an external organization provides and manages the other organization's entire business process(es) or functions(s) in a low cost location. Common examples are accounting, payroll and call centre operations.
Knowledge Process Outsourcing:	This is a **new enhancement** of Business Process Outsourcing, where external organizations provide domain based processes

and business expertise rather than just process expertise and requires advanced analytical and specialized skills from the outsourcing organization.

Application Service Provision: Where external organizations provide shared computer based services to customer organizations over a network. The complexities and costs of such shared software can be reduced and provided to organizations that could otherwise not justify the investment.

5.3.2.2 Supplier and Contact Database (SCD):

Figure 5.F – The Supplier and Contract Database

© Crown Copyright 2007 Reproduced under license from OGC

All Supplier Management process activity should be driven by supplier strategy and policy. In order to achieve consistency and effectiveness in the implementation of the policy, a Supplier and Contract Database (SCD) should be established.

Ideally the SCD should form an integrated element of a comprehensive CMS (Configuration Management System) or SKMS (Service Knowledge Management System), recording all supplier and contract details, together with the types of service, products etc. provided by each supplier, and all the other information and relationships with other associated CIs (Configuration Items). This will also contribute to the information held in the Service Portfolio and Catalog.

5.3.2.3 Relationships with other Lifecycle Phases:

The information within the SCD will provide a complete set of reference information for all Supplier Management procedures and activities needed across the Service Lifecycle. Such activities include:

Lifecycle Phase	Activities
Service Design	• Evaluating which components of service provision should/could be provided by an external supplier or partner • Supplier categorization and maintenance of the SCD • Evaluation and set-up of new suppliers and contracts
Service Design	• Assessing the transition to new suppliers • Establishing new suppliers
Service Operation	• Ongoing Supplier and Contract Management and performance • Contract renewal and termination
Continual Service Improvement	• Identifying improvement actions involving suppliers • Collating measurements gathered on supplier arrangements

This table shows that although Supplier Management is firmly placed within the Service Design Phase of the Lifecycle, many activities are carried out in the other Lifecycle Phases too.

5.3.3 Service Catalog Management

Imagine walking into a restaurant for lunch only to find there is no menu available for you to peruse. How will the staff provide you with information about what options are available to you? How will you know what ingredients and items are included with each meal? What will the price be of those meals? What about drinks or other items? Even if you manage to be served by a very efficient waiter who can recite everything to you flawlessly, how will you manage the large influx of information in such a small time and be able to choose what you want?

While this example may be far removed from the running of an IT organization the principles remain the same. A restaurant is in business to provide dining services to customers and through the use of their menu and the knowledge and skills of staff, customers can understand what is available to them and make effective choices in a simple manner. As an IT Service Provider we are in the business of providing IT services to our customers, but what mechanisms do we use to make these transactions simple yet effective for all parties?

For most IT organizations the Service Catalog provides this mechanism, and in many ways it serves as the foundation for much of the work involved within the scope of Service Offerings and Agreements. Without some agreed definition of what services we offer, what those services provide and which customers we provide them to, the development and management of Service Portfolios, Service Level Agreements, IT budgets and other related items become all the more difficult, and things only get worse as time progresses.

But it is not enough to simply have some form of Service Catalog. We must also seek to ensure that the Service Catalog is continually maintained and updated to contain correct, appropriate and relevant information to assist communication and transactions with customers.

5.3.3.1 Goal and objectives

The primary goal of Service Catalog Management is to ensure that a Service Catalog is produced, maintained and always contains accurate information on all operational services and those ready for deployment.

Other objectives include:

- To provide a single source of consistent information for communicating available services and their associated details, interfaces and dependencies
- To ensure that it is widely available to those who are approved to access it
- To enable mechanisms of self help-utilizing technology within the Service Catalog.

5.3.3.2 Scope

The scope of this process is to provide and maintain accurate information on all services that are being transitioned or have been transitioned to the live environment. This includes such tasks as:

- Definition of the service (what is being provided?)
- Production and maintenance of accurate Service Catalog information
- Development and maintenance of the interfaces and dependencies between the Service Catalog and Service Portfolio, ensuring consistency between the two items
- Identification and documentation of the interfaces and dependencies between all services (and supporting services) within the Service Catalog and Configuration Management System (CMS)
- Identification and documentation of the interfaces and dependencies between all services, supporting components and Configuration Items (CIs) within the Service Catalog and the CMS.

Depending on the number and complexity of services offered, the size of the customer and end user population and what objectives have been defined for the process, these activities and items may have little or a great deal of reliance on technology to be effective.

Once the definition of services and their interfaces is finalized, the knowledge and information of the Service Catalog is logically divided into two aspects:

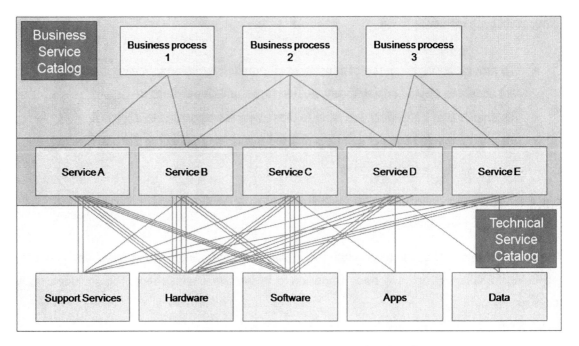

Figure 5.G: – The Business and Technical Service Catalogs

© Crown Copyright 2007 Reproduced under license from OGC

A Business Service Catalog: Which contains details of all the IT services defined in the context of customers, together with relationships to the business units and the business process they support. This information is utilized to form the customer view of the Service Catalog, using appropriate communication (language, use of business terminology, not overly technical) to ensure its effectiveness. In cases where the customer is an IT organization themselves then the technical level of detail provided should be appropriately expanded.

A Technical Service Catalog: Also contains details of all the IT services delivered to the customer, but by comparison, the Technical Service Catalogue includes records of the relationships that exist with other supporting services, shared services, components and Configuration Items necessary for the delivery of the service to the business. The Technical Service Catalog should underpin the Business Service Catalog, and is not always be visible to customers and users, unless specifically requested. In many cases the Technical Service Catalog itself is formed largely by the information contained within the Configuration Management System.

5.3.3.3   Developing the Service Catalog

While more extravagant implementations of the Service Catalog delivered via extensive internet/intranet solutions will maintain both aspects in an integrated fashion, less mature organizations may choose to maintain these separately. Regardless of the implementation method, the key requirement is that the desired information is easily accessible by the authorized parties and communicated in a form that is appropriate for the audience.

The starting point for any Service Catalog journey is to begin identifying what actual services are being provided and who are the customers of these services. While it sounds simple enough, for an organization with a long history and large amount of customers there will often be a lack of clarity in this regard, resulting in confusion and debate about what actually constitutes a service.

From an IT perspective, many staff will typically identify IT systems such as software or applications as being the service offered to customers. In other cases, the service will be seen to be composed of multiple services (which in turn are formed by one or more IT systems). In short, looking at services from only an IT perspective will lead you down a dangerous path and most likely cause you more headaches and grief in the process.

Instead, the recommended starting point is to look at things from the customer perspective. This is normally performed by asking customers what they perceive to be the IT Services they are utilizing and how they map onto and support their business processes. Just like the design of services should be coordinated in a top-down approach, so should the associated definition for inclusion in the Service Catalog. Regardless of exactly how this occurs, each organization needs to develop a policy defining what constitutes a service and how it is defined and agreed within their own organization.

The top-down approach may lead to the creation of a service hierarchy, qualifying types of services such as:

- **Business Services** – that what is actually used and seen by the customer
- **Supporting Services**, including further definition as:

- o Infrastructure Services
- o Application Services
- o Network Services
- o Data Management Services
- **Shared and Commodity Services**
- **Externally provided Services** – those provided/managed by an 3rd party organization.

As the definition of services begins to occur, consideration should be made as to who are the actual customers of these services. Eventually through a cycle of discussions with customers a clearer picture will emerge, providing the beginnings of a Business Service Catalog.

5.3.4 Capacity Management

5.3.4.1 Goal and objectives

The primary goal of Capacity Management is to ensure that cost-justifiable IT capacity in all areas of IT exists and is matched to the current and future agreed needs of the business in a timely manner.

Other objectives of Capacity Management are to:

- Produce and maintain an up to date Capacity Plan
- Provide advice and guidance
- Ensure service performance meets or exceeds agreed targets
- Assist with diagnosis and resolution of performance and capacity related incidents and problems
- Assess impact of all changes on the Capacity Plan, services and resources
- Ensure proactive measures to improve performance of service are implemented, where cost-justifiable.

Capacity Management provides the predictive and ongoing capacity indicators needed to align capacity to demand. It is about finding the right balance between resources and capabilities, and demand.

5.3.4.2 Principles of Capacity Management

Figure 5.H: – The balancing act of Capacity Management

In coordination with the processes of Financial Management and Demand Management, Capacity Management seeks to provide a continual optimal balance between supply against demand, and costs against resources needed.

This optimum balance is only achieved both now and in the future by ensuring that Capacity Management is involved in all aspects of the Service Lifecycle. When this doesn't occur Capacity Management only operates as a reactive process, with limited benefits being delivered as a result.

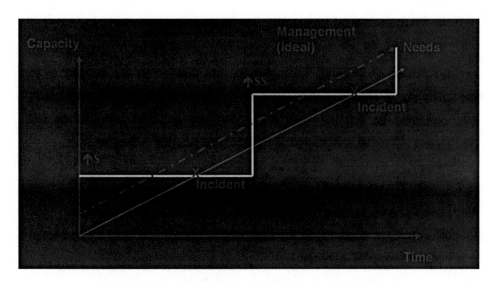

Figure 5:I: – Capacity Management when used reactively

In the above figure, capacity is only implemented when disruptions begin to occur as demand has exceeded supply. While the implemented capacity does work to resolve the disruptions, there are some consequences to this type of reactive behavior including:

- IT infrastructure components being purchased that don't optimally fit the requirements or architecture
- Budget overruns for the unforeseen and unanticipated purchases
- Periods of time where there are potentially large amounts of excess capacity
- Reduced customer and user satisfaction with the affected IT services
- A general negatively affected perception of the IT organization as a whole.

©The Art of Service

5.3.4.3 Sub-Processes of Capacity Management:

Some of the activities of Capacity Management are defined in the context of three sub-processes consisting of Business, Service and Component Capacity Management. Besides these, there will also be discussion of the operational activities required as well as the techniques that are utilized in various forms by the three different sub-processes.

Business Capacity Management:
- Manages Capacity to meet future business requirements for IT services
- Identifies changes occurring in the business to assess how they might impact capacity and performance of IT services
- Plans and implements sufficient capacity in an appropriate timescale
- Should be included in Change Management and Project management activities.

Service Capacity Management
- Focuses on managing ongoing service performance as detailed in the Service Level Agreements
- Establishes baselines and profiles of use of Services, including all components and sub-services that affect the user experience
- Reports to the Service Level Manager and Service Owner regarding end-to-end service capacity, performance and utilization.

Component Capacity Management
- Identifies and manages each of the individual components of the IT Infrastructure (e.g. CPU, memory, disks, network bandwidth, server load)
- Evaluates new technology and how it might be leveraged to benefit the organization
- Balances loads across resources for optimal performance of services.

All three sub-processes collate their data and for use by other ITSM processes, primarily Service Level Management and Financial Management.

5.3.4.4 Activities

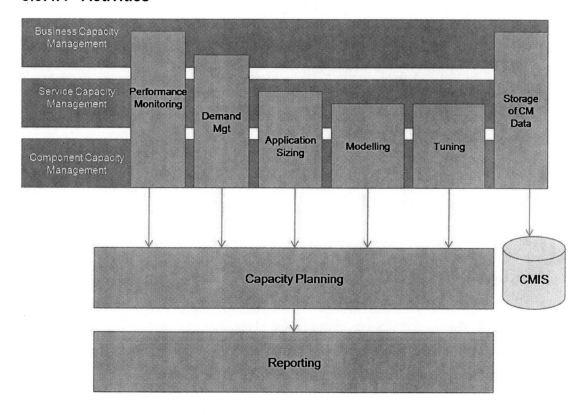

Figure 5.J – Activities of Capacity Management

© Crown Copyright 2007 Reproduced under license from OGC

Capacity Management consists of these main activities:

1. **Performance Monitoring** - Measuring, monitoring, and tuning the performance of IT services and the individual infrastructure components

2. **Demand Management** - Short term reactive implementation of strategies considered within Service Strategy to manage current demand

3. **Application Sizing** - Determining the hardware or application capacity required to support new or modified applications and their predicted workload.

4. **Modeling** - Used to forecast the behavior of the infrastructure under *certain conditions (e.g. what if the number of users doubled; what if a network segment fails)*

5. **Tuning** – Modifications made under the control of Change Management to enable better utilization of current infrastructure
6. **Storage of Capacity Management Data** – Storing all business, service and component capacity data to assist decision making within the Capacity Management and Financial Management processes
7. **Capacity Planning** – Forecasting when and where capacity will need to be increased and decreased. A formal Capacity Plan will document these recommendations
8. **Reporting.**

5.3.4.5 Roles and Responsibilities

Capacity Manager

Responsibilities:

- Ensure adequate performance and capacity for all IT services
- Capacity Plan (responsible for its development and management)
- Delegate responsibility for performance and capacity monitoring and alerting tasks
- Report provision and advice to other areas of IT and the business.

Skills: Strategic business awareness, technical, analytical, consultancy.

Capacity Management is critical for ensuring effective and efficient capacity and performance of IT Services and IT components in line with identified business requirements and the overall IT strategic objectives. It is essential that the Capacity Manager ensures that the process is appropriately integrated with all aspects of the Service Lifecycle.

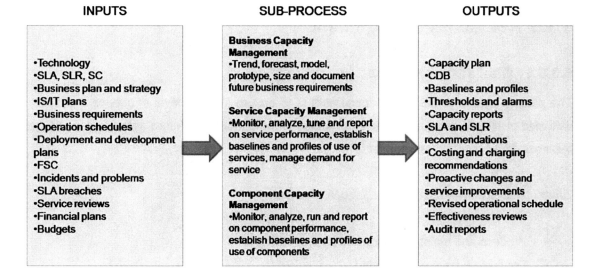

INPUTS	SUB-PROCESS	OUTPUTS

INPUTS
- Technology
- SLA, SLR, SC
- Business plan and strategy
- IS/IT plans
- Business requirements
- Operation schedules
- Deployment and development plans
- FSC
- Incidents and problems
- SLA breaches
- Service reviews
- Financial plans
- Budgets

SUB-PROCESS

Business Capacity Management
- Trend, forecast, model, prototype, size and document future business requirements

Service Capacity Management
- Monitor, analyze, tune and report on service performance, establish baselines and profiles of use of services, manage demand for service

Component Capacity Management
- Monitor, analyze, run and report on component performance, establish baselines and profiles of use of components

OUTPUTS
- Capacity plan
- CDB
- Baselines and profiles
- Thresholds and alarms
- Capacity reports
- SLA and SLR recommendations
- Costing and charging recommendations
- Proactive changes and service improvements
- Revised operational schedule
- Effectiveness reviews
- Audit reports

Figure 5.K – Interfaces of Capacity Management

5.3.5 Availability Management

5.3.5.1 Goal and objectives

The primary goal of Availability Management is to ensure that the level of service availability delivered in all services is matched to or exceeds the current and future agreed needs of the business, in a cost-effective manner.

Other objectives include providing the capabilities to:

- Produce and maintain an up-to-date Availability Plan
- Provide advice and guidance
- Ensure availability achievements meet or exceed agreed targets
- Assist with diagnosis and resolution of availability related incidents and problems
- Assess impact of all changes on the Availability Plan
- Ensure frequent proactive measures are taken to optimize and improve the availability of services are implemented where it is cost-justifiable.

Question:

Why could users be happy with a 60 minute outage and yet be unhappy with 30 minute outage?

1: 30min outage during peak time, overtime being paid to staff, urgent report required.

2: 60min outage on weekend, holiday, off peak, when service not required.

3: 30min outage on critical IT Service, 60min outage on non-critical IT Service.

4: 30mins unplanned outage, 60min planned outage (e.g. maintenance).

For a consumer/user of an IT Service, its Availability and Reliability can directly influence both the perception and satisfaction of the overall IT Service provision. However, when disruptions are properly communicated and managed effectively, the impact on the user population's experience can be significantly reduced.

5.3.5.2 Activities

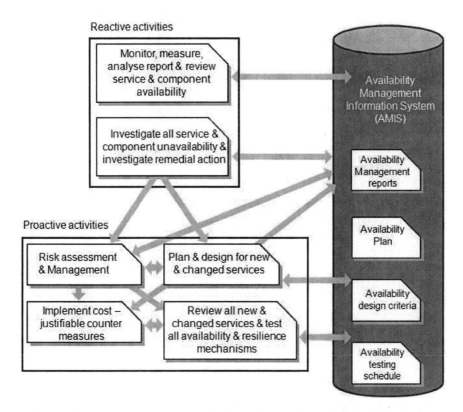

Figure 5.L: – The proactive and reactive elements of Availability Management

© Crown Copyright 2007 Reproduced under license from OGC

Proactive Activities (primarily executed in Service Design and Service Transition):

- The development and maintenance of an Availability Plan, which documents the current and future requirements for service availability, and the methods used to meet these requirements

- Development of a defined set of methods, techniques and calculations for the assessment and reporting of availability

- Liaison with IT Service Continuity Management and other aligned processes to assist with risk assessment and management activities

- Ensuring consistency in the design of services and components to align with the business requirements for availability.

Reactive Activities (primarily executed in Service Operation and Continual Service Improvement):

- Regular monitoring of all aspects of availability, reliability and maintainability, including supporting processes such as Event Management for timely disruption detection and escalation
- Regular and event-based reporting of service and component availability
- Ensuring regular maintenance is performed according to the levels of risk across the IT infrastructure
- Assessing the performance of and data gathered by various Service Operation processes such as Incident and Problem Management to determine what improvement actions might be made to improve availability levels or the way in which they are met.

5.3.5.3 Basic Concepts for Availability Management

The following concepts are fundamental to the understanding and application of Availability Management.

Terminology	Explanations
1. Availability	The ability of a service, component or CI to perform its agreed function when required. It is typically measured an reported as a percentage using the following formula: $$\text{Availability (\%)} = \frac{\text{Agreed Service Time} - \text{Downtime}}{\text{Agreed Service Time}} \times 100\ \%$$ This means that if a service is only partly functional, or the performance is degraded to a point outside of normal service operation, then the service should be classed as unavailable.
2. Service Availability	Involves all aspects of service availability and unavailability and the impact of component availability.

3. Component Availability	Involves all aspects of component availability and unavailability

4. Reliability

A measure of how long a service, component or CI can perform its agreed function without interruption. This metric provides an understanding of the frequency of disruption and is often reported as Mean Time Between Service Incidents (MTBSI) or Mean Time Between Failures (MTBF). It is typically calculated with the formulas:

$$\text{Reliability (MTBSI)} = \frac{\text{Available time in hours}}{\text{Number of service disruptions}}$$

$$\text{Reliability (MTBF)} = \frac{\text{Available time in hours} - \text{Total Downtime in hours}}{\text{Number of service disruptions}}$$

5. Maintainability

A measure of how quickly and effectively a service, component or CI can be restored to normal operation after a failure. This metric is typically measured and reported as the Mean Time to Restore Service (MTRS), which includes the entire time from the start of the disruption until the full recovery. The following formula is normally used:

$$\text{Maintainability (MTRS)} = \frac{\text{Total downtime in hours}}{\text{Number of service disruptions}}$$

EXAMPLE: For a service that is provided 24 x 7 and running for a reporting period of 5020 hours with only two disruptions (one of 6 hours and one of 14 hours), the following metrics would result:

$$\text{Availability (\%)} = \frac{5020 - 20}{5020} \times 100\% = 99.60\%$$

$$\text{Reliability (MTBSI)} = \frac{5020}{2} = 2510 \text{ hours}$$

$$\text{Reliability (MTBF)} = 5000 = 2500 \text{ hours}$$

$$\text{Maintainability (MTRS)} = \frac{20}{2} = 10 \text{ hours}$$

6. Serviceability	The ability of an external (third-party) supplier to meet the terms of their contract. Often this contract will include agreed levels of availability, reliability and/or maintainability for a supporting service or component.
7. Vital Business Function (VBF)	Defined business critical elements of a business process that are supported by an IT service. While many functions are supported by IT, we typically prioritize our efforts and resources around supporting the critical elements, including the use of redundant and highly resilient components. Certain VBFs may need special designs which are now used commonly in key infrastructure components (such as servers), which include the following four concepts.
8.High Availability	A characteristic of the IT service that minimizes or masks the effects of component failure to the users of a service.
9. Fault tolerance	The ability of a service, component or CI to continue to operate correctly after failure of a component part.
10.Continuous operation	An approach or design to eliminate planned downtime of an IT service. This may mean that individual components are disrupted during maintenance, but the IT service as a whole remains available.
11. Continuous availability	An approach or design to achieve theoretical 100% level of service availability. Multiple design factors will support this to occur, but more stringent requirements will also be assessed (e.g. environment).

5.3.5.4 Expanded Incident Lifecycle

An aim of Availability Management is to ensure the duration and impact from Incidents impacting IT Services are minimized, to enable business operations to resume as quickly as possible.

The expanded Incident lifecycle enables the total IT Service downtime for any given Incident to be broken down and mapped against the major stages that all Incidents go through.

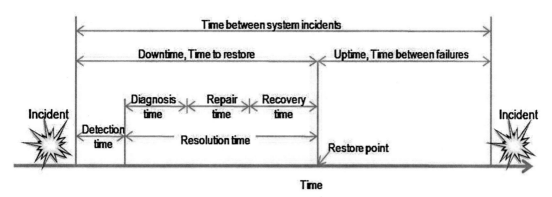

Figure 5.M – The Expanded Incident Lifecycle

© Crown Copyright 2007 Reproduced under license from OGC

Mean time between Failures (MTBF) or *uptime:*
- Average time between the recovery from one incident and the occurrence of the next incident, relates to the reliability of the service.

Mean time to Restore Service (MTRS) or *downtime:*
- Average time taken to restore a CI or IT service after a failure
- Measured from when CI or IT service fails until it is fully restored and delivering its normal functionality.

Mean time between System Incidents (MTBSI):

- Average time between the occurrences of two consecutive incidents
- Sum of the MTRS and MTBF.

Relationships of the above terms:

- High ratio of MTBF/MTBSI indicates there are frequently occurring minor faults or disruptions
- Low ratio of MTBF/MTBSI indicates there are infrequently occurring major faults or disruptions.

Elements making up the Mean Time to Restore Service (MTRS):

- **Detection Time:** Time for the service provider to be **informed** of the fault **(reported)**
- **Diagnosis Time:** Time for the service provider to respond after **diagnosis** completed
- **Repair Time:**
  - Time the service provider restores the components that caused the fault
  - Calculated from **diagnosis** to **recovery** time.
- **Restoration Time(MTRS):**
  - The **agreed** level of service is restored to the user
  - Calculated from **detection** to **restore point.**
- **Restore Point:** The point where the agreed level of service has been restored.

5.3.5.5 Roles and Responsibilities

Availability Manager

Responsibilities:

- Ensure adequate availability of all IT services
- Developing and maintaining an Availability Plan
- Oversee availability monitoring and improvement of the process
- Report provision and advice.

Skills: Awareness of how IT supports the business, technical, analytical, consultancy, seeks continuous improvement.

Note: The Availability Manager does not seek to achieve 100% Availability of all services and systems, but instead seeks to deliver Availability that matches or exceeds (within reason) the agreed business requirements.

5.3.5.6 Availability Management Metrics

Typical metrics for evaluation the effectiveness and efficiency of Availability Management include:

- Percentage reduction in unavailability of services and components
- Percentage increase in the reliability of services and components
- Effective review and follow up of all SLA, OLA and UC breaches
- Percentage improvement in overall end-to-end availability of service
- Percentage reduction in the number and impact of service breaks
- Improvement of MTBF
- Improvement of MTBSI
- Reduction in MTRS.

While the above list does include a number of important measures, the service provider should also seek to demonstrate the impact that availability/unavailability has on the business. Such examples of business oriented availability reporting include:

- User minutes lost due to disruption
- Transactions lost or delayed due to disruption
- Customer complaints caused by disruption.

5.3.6 IT Service Continuity Management

Goal: The primary goal of IT Service Continuity Management (ITSCM) is to support the overall *Business Continuity Management* practices of the organization by ensuring that the required IT Infrastructure, and the IT service provision, can be recovered within the required and agreed business time scales.

Other objectives include to:

- Maintain a set of IT Service Continuity Plans and IT recovery plans**
- Complete regular Business Impact Analysis (BIA) exercises
- Conduct regular Risk Analysis and Management
- Provide advice and guidance
- Ensure appropriate continuity and recovery mechanisms are in place
- Assess the impact of all changes on ITSCM plans and procedures
- Ensure that proactive measures to improve the recovery mechanisms for services are implemented
- Negotiate and agree on necessary contracts with suppliers (with Supplier Management).

** Often referred to as Disaster Recovery planning. **

Scope

The scope of ITSCM can be said to be focused on planning for, managing and recovering from "IT disasters". These disasters are severe enough to have a critical impact on business operations and as a result will typically require a separate set of infrastructure and facilities to recover. Less significant events are dealt with as part of the Incident Management process in association with Availability Management.

The disaster does not necessarily need to be a fire, flood, pestilence or plague, but any disruption that causes a severe impact to one or more business processes. Accordingly, the scope of ITSCM should be carefully defined according to the organization's needs, which may result in continuity planning and recovery mechanisms for some or all of the IT services being provided to the business.

There are longer-term business risks that are out of the scope of ITSCM, including those arising from changes in business direction, organizational restructures or emergence of new competitors in the market place. These are more the focus of processes such as Service Portfolio Management and Change Management.

So for general guidance, the recommended activities for any ITSCM implementation include:

- The agreement of the scope of the process and the policies adopted
- Business Impact Analysis (BIA) to quantify the impact a loss of IT service would have on the business
- Risk Analysis
- Production of an overall ITSCM strategy that must be integrated into the BCM strategy
- Production of ITSCM plans
- Testing of plans
- Ongoing education and awareness, operation and maintenance of plans.

Terminology	Explanation
Disaster:	NOT part of *daily operational activities* and requires a *separate system*. (Not necessarily a flood, fire etc. but may be due to a blackout or power problem and the SLAs are in danger of being breached).
Business Continuity Management: **(BCM)**	Strategies and actions to take place to continue Business Processes in the case of a disaster. It is essential that the ITSCM strategy is integrated into and a subset of the BCM strategy.
Business Impact Analysis: **(BIA)**	Quantifies the impact loss of IT service would have on the business.

Risk Assessment: Evaluate *Assets*, *threats* and *vulnerabilities* that exist to business processes, IT services, IT infrastructure and other assets.

5.3.6.1 Activities of IT Service Continuity Management

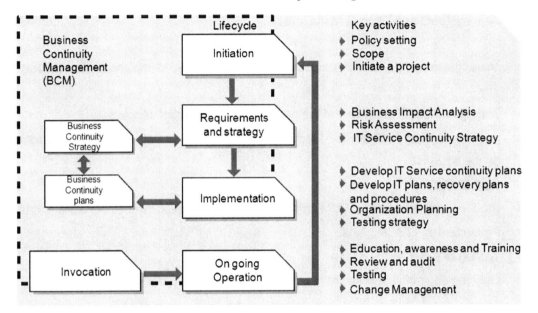

Figure 5.N – Activities of IT Service Continuity Management

© Crown Copyright 2007 Reproduced under license from OGC

Performing a Business Impact Analysis (BIA) identifies:

- Critical business processes & Vital Business Functions
- Potential damage or loss caused by disruption
- Possible escalations caused by damage or loss
- Necessary resources required to enable continuity of critical business processes
- Time constraints for minimum recovery of facilities and services
- Time constraints for complete recovery of facilities and services.

Risk Assessment:

- Gather information on assets (IT infrastructure components)
- Threats from both Internal & external sources (the likelihood of occurring)
- Vulnerabilities (the extent of impact or effect on organization).

Terminology	Explanation
Counter Measures:	Measures to prevent or *recover* from disaster
Manual Workaround:	Using *non-IT* based solution to overcome IT service disruption
Gradual recovery:	Aka *Cold* standby (>72hrs to recover from a 'Disaster')
Intermediate Recovery:	Aka *Warm* standby (24-72hrs to recover from a 'Disaster')
Immediate Recovery:	Aka *Hot* standby (< 24hrs, usually implies 1-2 hrs to recover from a 'Disaster)
Reciprocal Arrangement:	Agreement with another similar sized company to share disaster recovery obligations

©The Art of Service

5.3.6.2 Ongoing Operation

- Education & awareness
    - o Involving IT staff, customers, users, suppliers and other stakeholders.
- Training
- Reviews
- Ongoing testing
    - o At least annually
    - o Following major changes
- Audits of recovery procedures, risk-reduction measures and for compliance to procedures.
- Ensuring integration with Change Management, so that all changes are assessed as to their requirements for continuity and their potential impact on existing continuity strategies.

5.3.6.3 Roles and Responsibilities

Typical responsibilities for ITSCM in planning and dealing with disaster are similar to how First Aid Officers and Fire Wardens act in planning and operational roles (they may not be full-time roles, but are instead a 'hat' they wear when required). See the following table for an example of how responsibilities for ITSCM are typically assigned.

Role	Responsibilities
Board	• Crisis Management • Corporate/Business decisions • External affairs
Senior Mgmt	• Co-ordination • Direction and arbitration • Resource authorization
Management	• Invocation of continuity or recovery • Team Leadership • Site Management • Liaison and Reporting
Supervisors and Staff	• Task execution • Team membership • Team and Site liaison

Skill requirements for the ITSCM Manager and other involved staff include:

- Knowledge of the business (help to set priorities for protection and recovery)
- Calm under pressure
- Analytical (problem solving)
- Leadership and Team players
- Negotiation and Communication.

5.3.7 Information Security Management

5.3.7.1 Goal and objectives

To align IT security with business security and ensure that information security is effectively managed in all service and IT Service Management activities.

Security objectives are met when:

- Information is available and usable when required, and the systems that provide it can appropriate resist attacks and recover from or prevent failures (availability)
- Information is observed by or disclosed to only those who have a right to know (confidentiality)
- Information is complete, accurate and protected against unauthorized modification (integrity)
- Business transactions, as well as information exchanges between enterprises, or with partners, can be trusted (authenticity and non-repudiation).

Information Security Management ensures that the **confidentiality**, **integrity** and **availability** of an organization's assets, information, data and IT services is maintained. Information Security Management must consider the following four perspectives:

- Organizational – Define security policies and staff awareness of these
- Procedural – Defined procedures used to control security
- Physical – Controls used to protect any physical sites against security incidents
- Technical – Controls used to protect the IT infrastructure against security incidents.

5.3.7.2 Information Security Management Policy

A consistent set of policies and supporting documents should be developed to define the organization's approach to security, which is supported by all levels of management in the organization.

These policies should be made available to customers and users, and their compliance should be referred to in all SLRs, SLAs, contracts and agreements. The policies should be authorized by top executive management within the business and IT, and compliance to them should be endorsed on a regular basis. All security policies should be reviewed and, where necessary, revised on at least an annual basis.

The overall Information Security Policy should consist of a number of sub-components or sub-policies, covering:

- The use and misuse of IT assets
- Access control
- Password control
- E-mail
- Internet
- Anti-virus
- Information classification
- Document classification
- Remote access
- Supplier access
- Asset disposal.

The Information Security Management System (ISMS)

The ISMS contains the standards, management procedures and guidelines that support the Information Security Management policies. Using this in conjunction to an overall framework for managing security will help to ensure that the Four Ps of People, Process, Products, and Partners are considered as to the requirements for security and control.

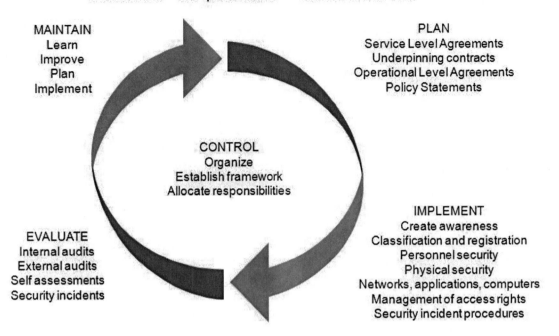

Figure 5.O: – Framework for managing IT security

© Crown Copyright 2007 Reproduced under license from OGC

As a guide, standards such as ISO 27001 provide a formal standard by which to compare or certify their own ISMS, covering the five main elements of:

1. *Plan*

Planning is used to identify and recommend the appropriate security measures that will support the requirements and objectives of the organization. SLAs and OLAs, business and organizational plans and strategies, regulation and compliance requirements (such as Privacy Acts) as well as the legal, moral and ethical responsibilities for information security will be considered in the development of these measures.

2. *Implement*

The objective of this element is to ensure that the appropriate measures, procedures, tools and controls are in place to support the Information Security Policy.

3. *Control*

The objectives of the control element of the ISMS are to:

- Ensure the framework is developed to support Information Security Management
- Develop an organizational structure appropriate to support the Information Security Policy
- Allocate responsibilities
- Establish and control documentation.

4. *Evaluate*

The evaluate element of the ISMS is focused on ensuring

- Regular audits and reviews are performed
- Policy and process compliance is evaluated
- Information and audit reports are provided to management and external regulators if required.

5. *Maintain*

As part of Continual Service Improvement, the maintain element seeks to:

- Improve security agreements as documented in SLAs and OLAs
- Improve the implementation and use of security measures and controls.

5.3.7.3 Activities

The activities of Information Security Management are involved in multiple phases of the Service Lifecycle, including the:

- Development and maintenance of the Information Security Policy
- Communication, implementation and enforcement of the security policies
- Assessment and classification of all information assets and documentation
- Implementation and continual review of appropriate security controls
- Monitoring and management of all security incidents
- Analysis, reporting and reduction of the volumes and impact of security breaches and incidents
- Scheduling and execution of security reviews, audits and penetration tests.

Training and awareness is particularly vital, and is often the weakness in an organization's control of security (particularly at the end-user stage). As part of the maintain element of the ISMS, consideration should be given as to methods and techniques that can be improved so that the policies and standards can be more easily followed and implemented.

5.3.7.4 Security Controls

The set of security controls should be designed to support and enforce the Information Security Policy and to minimize all recognized and potential threats. The controls will be considerably more cost effective if included within the design of all services. This ensures continued protection of all existing services and that new services are accessed in line with the policy.

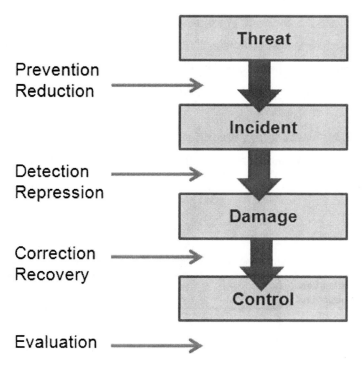

Figure 5.P: – Security Control

© Crown Copyright 2007 Reproduced under license from OGC

There are various security threats to our infrastructure and we want to prevent or reduce the damage of these as much as possible. Prevention/Risk reduction measures assist us to do this. E.G. Antivirus systems, firewalls etc.

1. In the case that they do pass our prevention mechanisms, we need to have detection techniques to identify when and where they occurred.
2. Once a security incident has occurred, we want to repress or minimize the damage associated with this incident. We then want to correct any damage caused and recover our infrastructure to normal levels. E.G. Antivirus systems quarantining an affected file.
3. After this process we need to review how and why the breach occurred and how successful were we in responding to the breach.

To assist in identifying what controls are missing or ineffective, a matrix can be developed that analyzes each of the control measures used for the different perspectives of security that need to be protected and controlled.

Perspectives

Measures	Organizational	Procedural	Technical	Physical
Prevention Reduction				
Detection				
Repression				
Correction				
Evaluation				

Figure 5.Q – Activities of Information Security Management

© Crown Copyright 2007 Reproduced under license from OGC

The Information Security Measure Matrix is a useful tool in performing a gap analysis:

- Ensures there is a balance in measures
- Avoids a concentration of measures in either a certain perspective (e.g. technical) or of a certain measure (e.g. detection).

Remember: ultimately it's a **cost-benefit analysis** that determines how much you invest in security.

5.3.7.5 Roles and Responsibilities

Information Security Manager

Responsibilities:

- Manage the entire security process
- Consult with senior management to agree on the Information Security Policy and gain support.

Skills: Strategic, public relations, tactical.

Security Officers

Responsibilities:

- Day to day operational duties to protect security levels
- Advise staff on security policy & measures.

Skills: Analytical, eye for detail, consultancy.

5.4 Service Design Summary

Good Service Design means it is possible to deliver quality, cost-effective services and to ensure that the business requirements are being met. It also delivers:

- Improved Quality of Service
- Improved Consistency of Service
- Improved Service Alignments
- Standards and Conventions to be followed
- More Effective Service Performance.

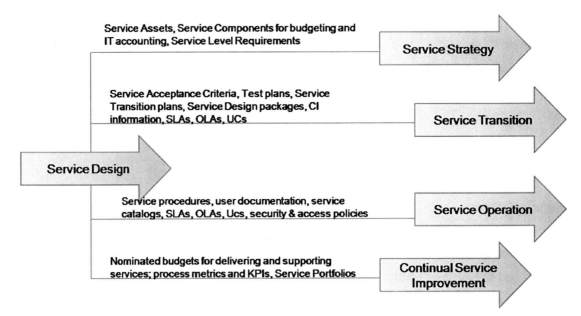

Figure 5.R – Some Service Design outputs to other lifecycle phases.

5.5 Service Design Scenario

Service Level Management Considerations

- SLR – detailed requirements that constitute the design criteria to be met e.g. secure, clear uninterrupted voice, real time video, accessible for novice users etc.
- SLA structure – decision made to develop multi-level structure (based on decision of service level package used, as well as offering greater security and accessibility to various departments/users).

Service Catalog Management Considerations

- Business Service Catalogue – will describe HYPE service as business understands it, including levels of service
- Technical Services Catalogue – will clearly list technical and supporting service information, e.g. ISP bandwidth, server requirements etc.

Supplier Management Considerations

- Negotiate UCs with software vendor, ISP, WAN
- Monitor external supplier service – discussions with Availability Management, Service Desk etc.

Capacity Management Considerations

- **Application Sizing** – assessing what minimum PC requirements needed to support new HYPE software, as well as type of webcam to best provide service, network bandwidth
- **Modeling** – how many users can videoconference before quality of service is affected – throughput/bandwidth targets? How may this service impact on other services?
- **Demand Management** – designing to ensure ability to limit bandwidth/video access during peak times for certain users/groups.

Availability Management Considerations

- To ensure availability targets are met, regular maintenance of components required, as well as ensuring through Supplier Management that ISP UC is met (serviceability requirements).

Information Security Management Considerations

- Confidentiality – user passwords design (e.g. HYPE service is not controlled locally – all information is stored on vendor's servers. If all users use same password as network login, resulting in a clear pattern, then it would be possible for security to be threatened if "someone" hacked into vendor server)
- Integrity – will logs of all conversations/messages/video kept be stored?
- Availability – having those logs available to those who require it, when they require it.

ITSCM Considerations

- The business has decided that this is a BCP, so standby arrangements are negotiated with business ($$)
- Decided that the telephone line and/or email will be possible recovery measures until service is restored – included in ITSCM plan.

The Service Design processes will ensure that HYPE meets the customer needs, can be developed and deployed by Service Transition, then maintained and supported within Service Operation.

5.6 Service Design Review Questions

Question 1

Which ITIL® process analyzes threats and dependencies to IT Services as part of the decision regarding "countermeasures" to be implemented?

    a)   Availability Management

    b)   IT Service Continuity Management

    c)   Problem Management

    d)   Service Asset & Configuration Management

Question 2

What is the name of the activity within the Capacity Management process whose purpose is to predict the future capacity requirements of new and changed services?

    a)   Application Sizing

    b)   Demand Management

    c)   Modeling

    d)   Tuning

Question 3

In which ITIL® process are negotiations held with customers about the availability and capacity levels to be provided?

    a)   Availability Management

    b)   Capacity Management

    c)   Financial Management for IT Services

    d)   Service Level Management

Question 4

Which of the following statements is false?

a) It is impossible to maintain user and customer satisfaction during a disruption to service.

b) When reporting the availability provided for a service, the percentage (%) availability that is calculated takes into account the agreed service hours.

c) Availability of services could be improved by changes to the architecture, ITSM processes or IT staffing levels.

d) Reports regarding availability should include more than just uptime, downtime and frequency of failure, and reflect the actual business impact of unavailability.

Question 5

Which of the following activities is Service Level Management responsible for?

a) Informing users of available services

b) Identifying customer needs

c) Overseeing service release schedule

d) Keeping accurate records of all configuration items

Question 6

Which process reviews Operational Level Agreements (OLAs) on a regular basis?

a) Supplier Management

b) Service Level Management

c) Service Portfolio Management

d) Contract Management

Question 7

What is another term for Uptime?

a) Mean Time Between Failures (MTBF)

b) Mean Time to Restore Service (MTRS)

c) Mean Time Between System Incidents (MTBSI)

d) Relationship between MTBF and MTBSI

Question 8

Which of the following is an activity of IT Service Continuity Management?

a) Advising end users of a system failure

b) Documenting the recovery procedure for a critical system

c) Reporting regarding availability

d) Guaranteeing that the Configuration Items are constantly kept up-to-date.

Question 9

Information security must consider the following four perspectives:

1. Organizational

2. Physical

3. Technical

4. ?

a) Process

b) Security

c) Procedural

d) Firewalls

Question 10

The 3 types of Service Level Agreements structures are:

a) Customer based, Service based, Corporate based

b) Corporate level, customer level, service level

c) Service based, customer based, user based

d) Customer based, service base, multi-level.

6 Service Transition

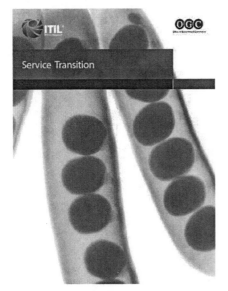

Figure 6.A: Service Transition

The Service Transition lifecycle phase focuses on the vulnerable transition between the Design phase and the Operation phase of a service. It is particularly critical as functional and technical errors not found during this phase will result in significantly higher impact levels to the business and/or IT infrastructure and will usually cost much more to fix once the Service is in operation.

Processes:
- Knowledge Management
- Service Asset and Configuration Management
- Change Management
- Release and Deployment Management
- Service Validation and Testing.

6.1 Objectives

The primary objective of Service Transition is the development and improvement of capabilities for transitioning new and modified services into operation.

Other objectives include:
- To ensure that new and changed services meet customer requirements and do not adversely impact the IT infrastructure or business processes
- To reduce the variation between estimated and actual costs, timeframes, risks and impact scales
- To build, configure, test and deploy quality Releases into operation in the most efficient manner while also minimizing disruption to the business and customers.

Effective Service Transition can significantly improve a Service provider's ability to effectively handle high volumes of change and releases across its Customer base. Other benefits delivered include:

- Increased success rate of Changes and Releases
- More accurate estimations of Service Levels and Warranties
- Less variation of costs and other resources against those estimated in budgets.

6.2 Service Transition Processes

6.2.1 Knowledge Management

The quality of decision making within the Service Lifecycle depends on the ability and understanding of those parties involved, the understanding of the benefits and consequences of actions taken, and the analysis of any of the surrounding issues involved. All of this in turn depends on the availability of accurate and timely knowledge, information and data, provided in a way that can be easily accessed and interpreted by the appropriate parties.

6.2.1.1 Goal and objectives

To enable organizations to improve the quality of management decision making by ensuring that reliable and secure information and data is available throughout the service lifecycle. The primary purpose is to improve efficiency by reducing the need to rediscover knowledge. This requires accessible, quality and relevant data and information to be available to staff.

The objectives of Knowledge Management are:

- Enabling the service provider to be more efficient and improve quality of service, increase satisfaction and reduce the cost of service
- Ensuring staff have a clear and common understanding of the value that their services provide to customers and the ways on which benefits are realized for the use of those services
- Ensuring that, at a given time and location, service provider staff have adequate information on:
    - Who is currently using their services
    - The current states of consumption
    - Service delivery constraints
    - Difficulties faced by the customer in fully realizing the benefits expected from the service.

6.2.1.2 Scope

While Knowledge Management is found, and primarily explained within the context of Service Transition, it is a process used by all elements of the Service Lifecycle to improve the decision making that occurs.

What is not considered to be within the scope of Knowledge Management is the detailed Configuration Item information that is captured and maintained by Service Asset and Configuration Management (but is interfaced with the same tools and systems).

6.2.1.3 Benefits

With particular focus on Service Transition, knowledge is one of the important elements that need to be transitioned as part of the service changes and associated releases being managed. Examples where successful transition requires effective Knowledge Management include:
- User, service desk, support staff and supplier understanding of the new or changed service, including knowledge of errors signed off before deployment, to facilitate their roles within that service
- Awareness of the use of the service, and the discontinuation of previous versions
- Establishment of the acceptable risk and confidence levels associated with the transition.

Outside of Service Transition, decision making at the strategic, tactical and operational levels all benefit from quality knowledge, information and data being available. Some benefits include:
- Optimized service portfolios (with appropriate balance of investments, resources, services and technology)
- Improved feedback loops between the design architects and the support staff for services
- Better real-time information and data for operational staff responding to user requests and incidents, as well as documented procedures for resolving known errors and requests.

6.2.1.4 Challenges faced by Knowledge Management

- Getting staff to use the systems
- Having the extra time required to record relevant information and knowledge after actions are made
- Managing information and knowledge that is no longer correct or relevant for the organization
- Designing a system that can scale well as an organization grows.

One of the more difficult components of Knowledge Management is ensuring that we do more than simply capture discrete facts about various elements of the organization and IT infrastructure. What this requires is an understanding of the different components and processes required to develop and mature knowledge and wisdom.

6.2.1.5 Data, Information, Knowledge, Wisdom (DIKW)

Knowledge Management is usually seen within the context of the DIKW structure seen below.

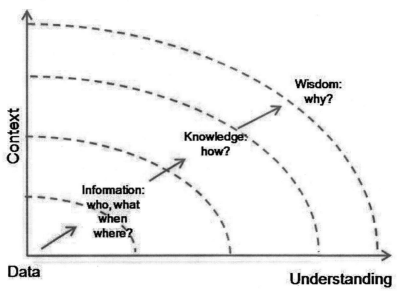

Figure 6.B: Moving from data to wisdom

© Crown Copyright 2007 Reproduced under license from OGC

Data:

Data is a set of discrete facts. Most organizations capture significant amounts of data every day. Knowledge Management activities seek to improve the capabilities for capturing, analyzing, synthesizing data and transforming it into information.

Information:

Information comes from providing context to data. This usually requires capturing various sources of data and applying some meaning or relevance to the set of facts. Knowledge Management focuses on measures for capturing, finding and reusing information so that work is not duplicated.

Knowledge:

Knowledge is composed of the experiences, ideas, insights and judgments from individuals and from their peers'. This usually requires the analysis of information, and is applied in such a way to facilitate decision making.

Wisdom:

The ultimate discernment of the material and having the application and contextual awareness to provide a strong common sense judgment. The use of wisdom ultimately enables an organization to direct its strategy and growth in competitive market spaces.

We can use tools and databases to capture Data, Information and Knowledge, but Wisdom cannot be captured this way, as Wisdom is a concept relating to abilities to use knowledge to make correct judgments and decisions.

6.2.1.6 Service Knowledge Management System (SKMS)

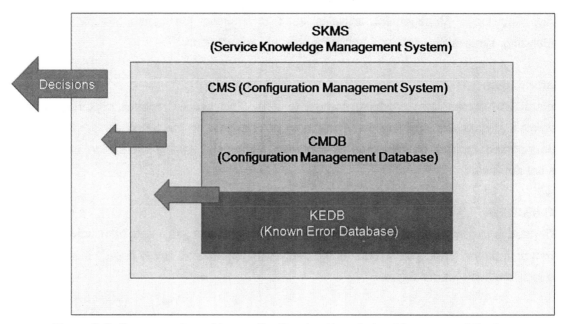

Figure 6.C: Components making up the Service Knowledge Management System

The SKMS describes the complete set of tools and databases that are used to manage knowledge and information, including the Configuration Management System as well as other tools and databases. The SKMS stores, manages, updates and presents all information that an IT service provider needs to manage the full lifecycle of its services. The main purpose of the SKMS is to provide quality information so that informed decisions can be made by the IT service provider.

Whereas the CMS focuses on providing information relating to the configuration of the IT infrastructure, the SKMS has a broader scope (as implied by the diagram) which includes anything pertaining to the needs of service management, including:

- Experience of staff
- Records of peripherals
- Supplier and Partner requirements and abilities
- Typical and anticipated user skill levels.

6.2.2 Service Asset and Configuration Management

6.2.2.1 Goal and objectives

The goal of Service Asset and Configuration Management is to support the agreed IT service provision *by managing, storing, controlling and providing information* about Configuration Items (CIs) and Service Assets throughout their life cycle. Quality and timely information supplied about CIs and Service Assets will enhance the effectiveness and efficiency of other Service Management processes, and in particular, those used within Service Transition.

Other objectives include:
- To support the business and customer's control objectives and requirements
- To minimize the number of quality and compliance issues caused by improper configuration of services and assets
- To optimize the service assets, IT configurations, capabilities and resources.

Terminology	Explanations
Configuration Item (CI):	*Reference to ANY* component that supports an IT service (except people). *Example: IT components or associated items such as Request for Changes, Incident Records, Service Level Agreements.*
Attribute:	*Specific* information about CIs that are appropriate to maintain. *Example: Size of RAM, hard drive, bandwidth*
CI Level:	Recording and reporting of CIs at the level that the *business requires* without being overly complex. It's a trade-off balancing the value that the information will provide versus the effort and cost to manage the information over time *(not too much or too little).*
Status Accounting:	Reporting of all *current and historical* data about each CI throughout its lifecycle. *Example: Status = Under Development, live, withdrawn etc.*

Configuration Baseline: Configuration details captured at a specific point in time. This captures both the structure and details of a configuration, and is used as a reference point for later comparison (e.g. After major changes, disaster recovery etc)

6.2.2.2 The Configuration Management Database (CDMB)

The CMDB is a set of one or more connected databases and information sources that provide a logical model of the IT infrastructure. It captures Configuration Items (CIs) and the relationships that exist between them. Figure 6.D demonstrates the elements of a CMDB.

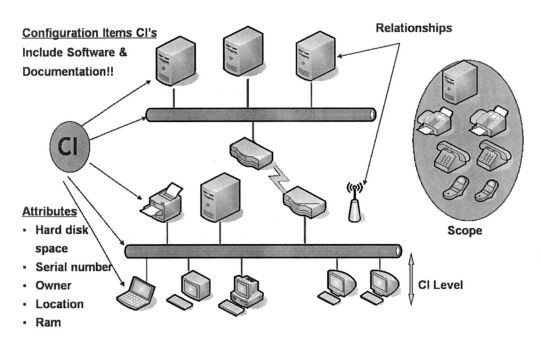

Figure 6.D – The Configuration Management Database (CMDB)

As shown, it is important to determine what level to which the CMDB will record information about the IT infrastructure and to decide what is not covered within the scope of the CMDB. Components out of scope are those typically not under the control of Change Management (e.g. telecommunication equipment). The CMS is also used for a wide range of purposes, including business processes where information is required for financial, compliance, HR or other reasons.

At the data level, the CMS may be formed by a combination of physical Configuration Management Databases (CMDBs), as well as other sources they feed and interface information together. Wherever possible, the CMS should provide access to information for other inventories rather than duplicating the data captured. Automation is a factor for success for larger CMS deployments, with discovery, inventory, audit, network management and other tools being used with interfaces to the CMS.

6.2.2.3 Activities

Figure 6.E – Configuration Management Activities

Notice how management and planning are the central activities. Good, sound Service Asset and Configuration Management requires thorough planning for the operation of the process to work.

Planning:
- Defining the strategy, policy, scope, objectives, processes and procedures for Service Asset and Configuration Management
- Roles and responsibilities of involved staff and stakeholders

- Location of storage areas and libraries used to hold hardware, software and documentation
- CMDB Design
- CI naming conventions
- Housekeeping including license management and archiving of CIs.

Identification:

The selection, identification, labelling and registration of CIs. It is the activity that determines what CIs will be recorded, what their attributes are, and what relationships exist with other CIs. Identification can take place for:

- Hardware and Software – include OS
- Business systems – custom built
- Packages – off the shelf
- Physical databases
- Feeds between databases and links
- Configuration baselines
- Software releases
- Documentation.

Control:

Where the CMDB is utilized to store or modify configuration data. Effective control ensures that only authorized and identifiable CIs are recorded from receipt to disposal in order to protect the integrity of the CMDB. Control occurs anytime the CMDB is altered, including:

- Registration of all new CIs and versions
- Update of CI records and licence control
- Updates in connection with RFCs and Change Management
- Update the CMDB after periodic checking of physical items.

Status Accounting:

The reporting of all current and historical data concerned with each CI throughout its lifecycle. Provides information on:

- Configuration baselines
- Latest software item versions
- The person responsible for status change
- CI change/incident/problem history.

Verification and Audit:

Reviews and audits verify the existence of CIs, checking that they are correctly recorded in the CMDB and that there is conformity between the documented baselines and the actual environment to which they refer.

Configuration Audits should occur at the following times:

- Before and after major changes to the IT infrastructure
- Following recovery from disaster
- In response to the detection of an unauthorized CI
- At regular intervals.

6.2.2.4 Benefits

The majority of benefits enabled by effective Service Asset and Configuration Management can be seen in improvements of other Service Management processes. By having quality asset and configuration data available, the benefits to other processes include:

- Better forecasting and planning of changes
- Changes and releases to be assessed planned and delivered successfully
- Incidents and problems to be resolved within the service level targets
- Changes to be traceable from requirements
- Enhanced ability to identify the costs for a service.

Benefits that may be seen to be provided primarily by the process alone include:

- Better adherence to standards
- Greater compliance to legal and regulatory obligations
- Optimum software licensing by ensuring correlation between licenses needed against the number of purchases
- The data about CIs and methods of controlling CIs is consolidated -> reduces auditing effort
- Opens opportunities for consolidation in CIs to support services.

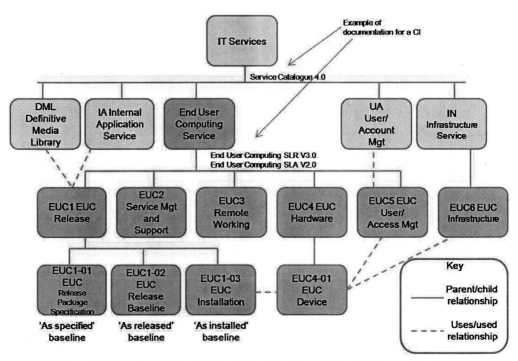

Figure 6.F – Example configuration breakdown for an IT Service

6.2.2.5 Roles and Responsibilities

Service Asset Management:

The management of service assets across the whole lifecycle including:

- Full lifecycle management of IT and service assets from acquisitions to disposal
- Maintenance of the asset inventory.

Configuration Management:

- To provide a logical model of the services, assets and infrastructure by recording the relationships between service assets and configuration items
- To ensure control procedures are complied with to protect the integrity of Configurations
- To support the information needs of other ITIL® processes.

The actual roles related to Service Asset and Configuration Management include:

- Service Asset Manager
- Configuration Manager
- Configuration Analyst
- Configuration Administrator/Librarian
- CMS/Tools Administrator
- Change Manager (all Changes to CIs must be authorized by Change Management).

6.2.3 Change Management

The ability to control and manage Changes to defined IT services and their supporting elements is viewed as a fundamental part of quality service management. When reviewing the typical strategic objectives of an IT service provider, most of these are underpinned by the requirement of effective Change control. These include strategies focusing on time-to-market, increased market share or high availability and security platforms, all of which require a controlled process by which to assess, control and manage Changes with varying levels of rigor.

Changes arise for a number of reasons:

- From requests of the business or customers, seeking to improve services, reduce costs or increasing ease and effectiveness of delivery and support
- From internal IT groups looking to proactively improve services or to resolve errors and correct service disruption.

The process of Change Management typically exists in order to:

- Optimize risk exposure (defined from both business and IT perspectives)
- Minimize the severity of any impact or disruption
- Deliver successful Changes at the first attempt.

To deliver these benefits while being careful not to cause excessive delays or bottlenecks as part of a coordinated approach to Service Transition, it is important to consider the diverse types of Changes that will be assessed, and how a balance can be maintained in regards to the varying needs and potential impacts of Changes. In light of this, it is important to interpret the following Change Management guidance with the understanding that is intended to be scaled to suit the organization, and the size, complexity and risk of Changes being assessed.

6.2.3.1 Goal and objectives:

To ensure that **standardized methods and procedures** are used for controlled, efficient and prompt handling of all Changes, in order to **minimize the impact** of Change-related Incidents upon service quality, and consequently to improve the day-to-day operations of the organization.

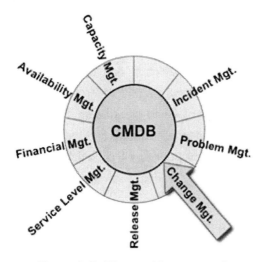

Change Management acts as the greatest contributor to the CMDB, as Changes to CMDB must be assessed and authorized by Change Management first.

To work effectively, Change Management needs to remain impartial to the needs of any one particular IT group or customer, in order to make effective decisions that best support the overall organizational objectives.

Figure 6.G: Change Management

6.2.3.2 Scope

The term Change is has many meanings, however the best definition of a service change is:

"Any alteration in the state of a Configuration Item (CI). This includes the addition, modification or removal of approved, supported or baselined hardware, network, software, application, environment, system, desktop build or associated documentation."

It is important that every organization defines those changes which lie outside the scope of their service change process (such as operational or business process and policy changes).

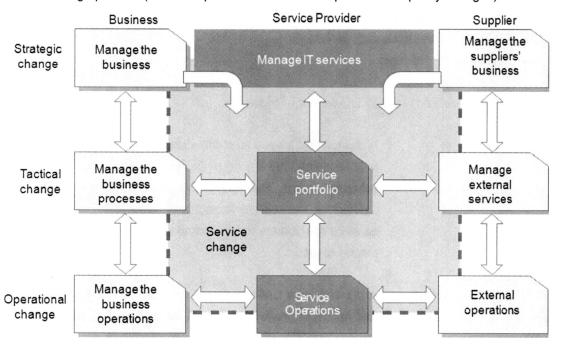

Figure 6.H: Scope of Change Management for IT Services

The figure demonstrates the typical scope of the Change Management process for an IT Service Provider and how it interfaces with the business and suppliers at strategic, tactical and operational levels. As discussed in Service Strategy, Service Portfolios provides the clear definition of all planned, current and retired services.

"Remember: Not every change is an improvement, but every improvement is a change!"

6.2.3.3 Change Models

The definition of different process models will allow an organization to maintain a balance between providing an appropriate level of control for changes without causing bottlenecks or restricting business growth. Change Models defines how various categories of changes are assessed and authorized, with different mechanisms and activities used to process and deliver changes based on the change type. The defined Change Models should also include:

- What steps should be taken to manage the change
- Roles and Responsibilities
- Timescales and thresholds for actions
- Escalation procedures.

Change Models defined within ITIL include the following:

NORMAL Change: A change that follows all of the steps of the change process. It is assessed by either a Change Manager or Change Advisory Board. Normal Changes will often be further defined by the relative impact and complexity, which will escalate the Change for assessment to the most appropriate person or group.

STANDARD Change: A *pre-approved* Change that is low risk, relatively common and follows a procedure or work instruction. E.g. password reset or provision of standard equipment to a new employee. RFCs are not required to implement a Standard Change, and they are logged and tracked using a different mechanism, such as a *service request.* While standard changes are effectively pre-approved by Change Management, they may still require forms of authorization such as other groups such Human Resources (HR) or Financial departments.

The main elements of a standard change are that:
- Authority is effectively given in advance

- The tasks are well known, documented and proven
- There is a defined trigger to initiate the Request For Change (RFC)
- Budgetary approval is typically defined or controlled by the requester
- The risk is usually low and always well understood

Over time and as the IT organization matures the list of standard changes should increase in order to maintain optimum levels of efficiency and effectiveness.

EMERGENCY Change: A change that must be introduced as soon as possible. E.g. to resolve a major incident or implement a security patch.

The change management process will normally have a specific procedure for handling Emergency Changes quickly, without sacrificing normal management controls. Organizations should be careful to ensure that the number of emergency changes be kept to a minimum, because they are typically more disruptive and prone to failure.

To enable this to occur, methods of assessment and documentation are typically modified, with some documentation occurring after the change has occurred.

6.2.3.4 Activities:

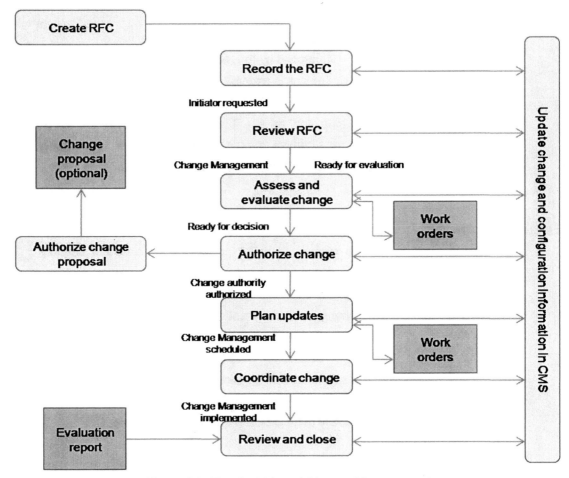

Figure 6.I– The Activities of Change Management

© *Crown Copyright 2007 Reproduced under license from OGC*

Where can RFCs be initiated?

Anywhere (Other ITIL processes, customers, end-users etc.)

Who does the actual build/test/implement?

- Technical areas
- Project Teams
- Release and Deployment Management.

Important Steps:

1. The RFC is logged
2. An initial review is performed (to filter RFCs)
3. The RFCs are assessed – may require involvement of CAB or ECAB
4. This is authorized by the Change Manager
5. Work orders are issued for the build of the Change (carried out by other groups)
6. Change Management coordinates the work performed (with multiple checkpoints)
7. The Change is reviewed (Post Implementation Review)
8. The Change is closed.

6.2.3.5   Assessing and Evaluating Changes

To ensure that the Change Management process does not become a bottleneck, it is important to define what Change Models will be used to ensure effective and efficient control and implementation of RFCs.

Level	Change Authority	Potential Impact/Risk
1	Business Executive Board.	High cost/risk change - Executive decision
2	The IT Management (Steering) Board	Change impacts multiple services/ organizational divisions
3	Change Advisory Board (CAB) or Emergency CAB (ECAB)	Change impacts only local/ service group
4	Change Manager	Change to a specific component of an IT Service
5	Local Authorization	Standard Change

6.2.3.6 The 7Rs of Change Management:

When assessing Changes, it is important to have answers to the following seven questions:

- Who RAISED the change?
- What is the REASON for the change?
- What is the RETURN required from the change?
- What are the RISKS involved in the change?
- What RESOURCES are required to deliver the change?
- Who is RESPONSIBLE for the build, test and implementation of the change?
- What is the RELATIONSHIP between this change and other changes?

These questions must be answered for **all changes**. Without this information the impact assessment cannot be completed, and the balance of risk and benefit to the live service will not be understood. This could result in the change not delivering all the possible or expected business benefits or even of it having a detrimental, unexpected effect on the live service.

6.2.3.7 Authorization of Changes

While the responsibility for authorization for Changes lies with the Change Manager, they in turn will ensure they have the approval of three main areas:
- Financial Approval - What's it going to cost? And what's the cost of not doing it?
- Business Approval - What are the consequences to the business? And not doing it?
- Technology Approval - What are the consequences to the infrastructure? And not doing it?

Key Points:
- Change Management should consider the implications of performing the Change, as well as the impacts of NOT implementing the Change
- Importance of empowering Change Manager as their primary role is to protect the integrity of the IT infrastructure.

6.2.3.8 Relationship with Project Management:

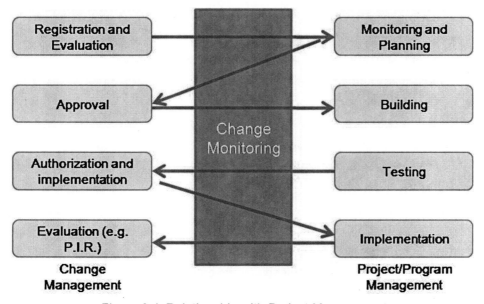

Figure 6.J: Relationship with Project Management

How does Change Management work with Project Management?

- Change Management authorizes, controls, coordinates, but *does not* plan, build, test or implement changes itself
- Change Management is concerned with Remediation Planning to ensure that each RFC has a fallback / rollback plan.

6.2.3.9 Roles and Responsibilities

Change Manager

- Administration of all RFCs
- Prepare RFCs for CAB meetings, communicate Change Schedule for Service Desk
- Authorize (or reject) changes.

CAB
- Advises Change Manager on authorization issues for RFCs with significant or major impact
- Typical representatives for a CAB under normal conditions are:
  o The Change Manager (chairs the CAB)
  o Customer representatives
  o User management
  o Application Developers/Supporters
  o Technical Experts and Consultants
  o Other Services Staff
  o Vendors and Suppliers.

Rather than having a static list of members, the CAB should include both static and dynamic members who will attend based on the needs for the changes being discussed.

Release and Deployment Manager
- Manages the release of changes
- Advises the Change Manager (as part of CAB) on release issues.

Technical specialists
- Build, test and deploy the actual hardware and software change components.

6.2.3.10   Change Management Metrics

It is important that a balanced view of metrics is used when assessing the effectiveness and efficiency of the Change Management process. These metrics include:
- Number of RFCs (Accepted/Rejected)
- Number and % of successful Changes
- Emergency Changes
- Number of Changes awaiting implementation
- Number of implemented Changes
- Change backlogs and bottle-necks
- Business impact of changes
- Frequency of Change to CIs.

6.2.3.11   Challenges affecting Change Management

- Change in culture – Now one central process comes into place that influences everyone's activities
- Bypassing - projects ducking the Change Management planning
- Optimal link with Configuration Management - to execute a controlled change all data MUST be reliable
- Commitment of the supplier(s) to the process
- Commitment of senior management.

6.2.4 Release and Deployment Management

Often forgotten or ignored in many IT Service Management implementations or initiatives, Release and Deployment can be mistakenly seen as the poor cousin of Change Management, of less importance and priority to both the business and IT organizations.

Much of the confusion and misunderstanding is perpetuated by the idea that Release and Deployment only focuses on the actual distribution of changes to the live environment. While timely and accurate distribution is indeed a goal of the process, the actual scope includes all of the activities, systems and functions required to build, test and deploy a release into product and enable effective handover to service operations.

In conjunction with the use of Change Management, Release and Deployment will enhance an organization's capabilities to develop, compile, reuse, distribute and rollback releases in accordance with defined policies that improve efficiency and reduce business disruption.

6.2.4.1 Goal and objectives

To deploy new releases into production, transition support to service operation, and enable its effective use in order to deliver value to the customer.

Other objectives of Release and Deployment are:
- To define and agree upon Release policies, and Release and Deployment plans with customers and stakeholders
- Ensure the integrity of constructed release packages and that they are recorded accurately in the Configuration Management System (CMS)
- Ensure that all release packages can be tracked, installed, verified, uninstalled or backed out if necessary
- Ensure the required skills and knowledge is transferred to support staff, customers, end users, suppliers and any other relevant stakeholders
- There is minimal unpredicted impact on the production services, customers and service operations.

Terminology	Explanations
Release:	A collection of **authorized** Changes to an IT Service.
Release Package:	A release package may be a single release unit or a structured set of release units, including the associated user or support documentation that is required.
Release Unit	A Release Unit describes the portion of a service of IT infrastructure that is normally released together according to the organization's release policy. The unit may vary depending on type(s) or item(s) of service asset or service component such as hardware or software.
Definitive Media Library (DML): *(previously known as the DSL)*	The secure library in which the definitive authorized versions of all media CIs are stored and protected. The DML should include definitive copies of purchased software (along with license documents or information) as well as software developed on site.

Definitive Spares (DS): *(previously known as DHS)*

Physical storage of all *spare IT components and assemblies maintained at the same level as within the live environment*. New IT assemblies are stored here until ready for use, and additional components can be used when needed for additional systems or in the recovery from Incidents.

- Details recorded in the CMDB, but controlled by Release and Deployment Management.

Early Life Support

Where release and deployment teams assist in managing any calls, incidents and problems that are detected in the immediate few days/weeks after the deployment of the new or modified service.

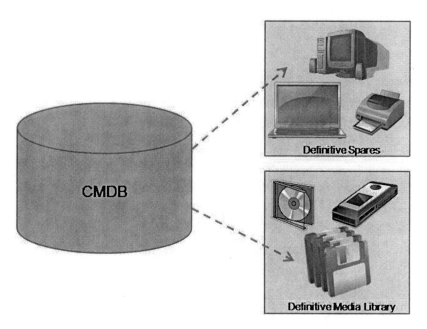

Figure 6.K – The Definitive Media Library and Definitive Spares

Remember – the elements found within the DML and DS are recorded as Configuration Items in the Configuration Management System.

Release and Deployment Management also works closely with Change Management and the Service Desk to inform users of scheduled changes/deployments. Tools used to do this can include:

- E-mail notification
- SMS notification
- Verbal communication.

6.2.4.2 Options for the deployment of Releases

Big Bang:
The new or changed service is deployed to all user areas in one operation. This will often be used when introducing an application change and consistency of service across the organization is considered important.

The negative aspect of the Big Bang approach is that it increases the risk and impact of a failed Release.

Phased Approach:
The service is deployed to a part of the user base initially, and then this operation is repeated for subsequent parts of the user base via a scheduled rollout plan.

This will be the case in many scenarios such as in retail organizations for new services being introduced into the stores' environment in manageable phases.

The Push Approach:
Used where the service component is deployed from the centre and pushed out to the target locations.

In terms of service deployment, delivering updated service components to all users, either in big bang or phased form is using the push approach, since the new or changed service is delivered into the users' environment at a time not of their choosing.

The Pull Approach:

Used for software releases where the software is made available in a central location but users are free to pull the software down to their own location at a time of their choosing or when a workstation restarts.

Automated:

The use of technology to automate Releases. This helps to ensure repeatability and consistency. The time required to provide a well-designed and efficient automated mechanism may not always be available or viable.

Manual:

Using manual activities to distribute a Release. It is important to monitor and measure the impact of many repeated manual activities as they are likely to be inefficient and error prone.

6.2.4.3 Release Policy

A Release Policy is the formal documentation of the overarching strategy for releases and was derived from the Service Design phase of the Service Lifecycle. It is the governing policy document for the process and must accommodate the majority of releases being implemented. Typical contents of a Release Policy include:

- Level of infrastructure to be controlled by Releases
- Preferred structure and schedules for Release Packages
- Definition of major and minor releases, emergency fixes
- Expected deliverables for each type of Release
- Policy on the production and execution of back out plans
- How and where Releases should be documented
- Blackout windows for releases based on business or IT requirements
- Roles and responsibilities defined for the Release and Deployment process
- Supplier contacts and escalation points.

6.2.4.4 Release and Deployment Activities

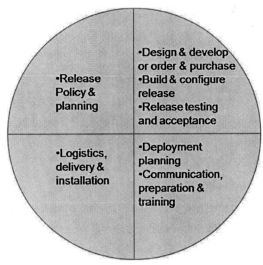

Key Points:

The Release Policy is the overarching strategy for Releases and was derived from the Service Design phase of the Service Lifecycle.

The Release Plan is the operational implementation for each release.

The Deployment Plan is the documented approach for distributing a single Release.

Figure 6.L: Phases and activities of Release and Deployment

Overview of Important Steps:

1. Release planning
2. Preparation for build, test and deployment
3. Build and test
4. Service test and pilots
5. Plan and prepare for deployment
6. Perform transfer. Deployment and retirement
7. Verify deployment
8. Early Life Support
9. Review and close the deployment
10. Review and close Service Transition.

Release Planning:

- Defining the Release contents
- Defining the Release Schedule
- Defining the resources, roles and responsibilities required for the Release

Build and Test: (Coordinates with other Service Design and Service Transition Processes):

- Produce Release assembly and build instructions
- Create Installation scripts
- Run Test plans
- Develop Back-out procedures
- Produce tested installation procedures.

Plan and Prepare for Deployment:

- Defining timetable for distribution
- Identification of affected CIs
- Defining communication plans
- Defining training plans
- Communication and training for:
  - Users
  - Support staff (including the Service Desk).

Perform Transfer. Deployment and Retirement:

During the actual implementation itself, the activities performed can be grouped under the following tasks:

1. Transfer financial assets
2. Transfer changes required to business/organization
3. Deploy processes and materials
4. Deploy Service Management Capability
5. Transfer service
6. Deploy service
7. Decommissioning and service retirement
8. Remove redundant assets.

These activities will need to be modified to accommodate any items specified in the deployment plan as part of the acceptance criteria for 'go live'.

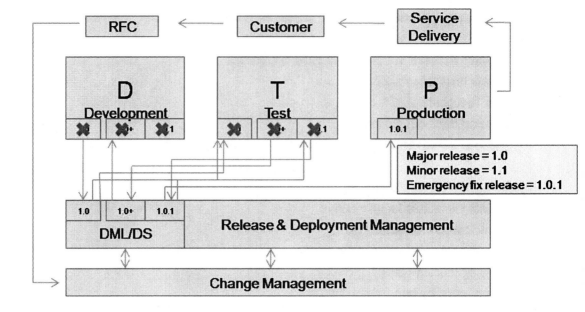

Figure 6.M - Transitioning New and Changed Services into Operation

Note how Change Management, Release and Deployment Management and Service Asset and Configuration Management work together for the transition of new or modified Services.

6.2.4.5 Roles and Responsibilities

Release and Deployment Manager
- Drive effectiveness and efficiency of process
- Manage entire release management team
- Liaise with Change and Configuration Management, IT platform managers, Application Developers etc.

Skills: technical and coordination skills, project manager.

Release and Deployment Management Team
- Manage the DML and DS
- Design, build, test and deploy releases
- Manage software management/distribution tools.

6.3 Service Transition Summary

Effective Service Transition can significantly improve a Service Provider's ability to effectively handle high volumes of change and releases across its Customer base. Other benefits delivered include:

- Increased success rate of Changes and Releases
- More accurate estimations of Service Levels and Warranties
- Less variation of costs against those estimated in budgets
- Less variation from resources plans.

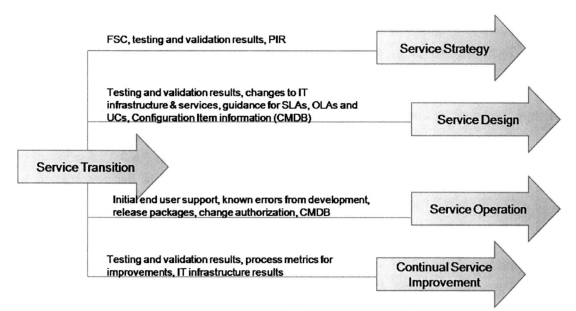

Figure 6.N – Some Service Transition outputs to other lifecycle phases

6.4 Service Transition Scenario

Knowledge Management Considerations
- If your SKMS is established, you would be able to identify if you have the skills required to support videoconferencing, for example.
- The SKMS will also help to determine the team required to build, test and deploy HYPE.
- Place to record and transfer user and support documentation.

Service Asset and Configuration Management Considerations
- HYPE software is registered as CI and relationships between it and the other CIs are known if…when… an incident occurs. This will assist to speed up resolution times.
- Decision made as to whether webcams are CIs themselves or an attribute of the PC/laptop it is attached to.

Change Management Considerations
- Ensure that the introduction of this new service minimizes impact on other services e.g. through testing, it is found that the RAM required slows down the PC, affecting other business critical apps. Change Management will assist with decision making to determine best path of action (through CAB).

Release and Deployment Management Considerations
- Builds and tests HYPE – decision here to limit video resolution to minimize bandwidth.
- Stores original authorized software in DML
- Ensures that design aspects are adhered to when building (e.g. ensuring that the password policies are adhered to
- Organizes training on using HYPE – (priority given to Service Desk 1st and pilot users).

6.5 Service Transition Review Questions

Question 1

The key element of a standard change is?

    a) Documentation of a pre-approved procedure for implementing the change

    b) Low risk to the production environment

    c) No requirement for service downtime

    d) It can be included in the next monthly or quarterly release

Question 2

Release and deployment options include:

1. Big bang vs. Phased

2. Automated vs. Manual

3. ?

    a) Push vs. Proposed

    b) Push vs. Pull

    c) Requested vs. Forced

    d) Proposed vs. Forced

Question 3

The 4 spheres of knowledge management are:

    a) Data, facts, knowledge, wisdom

    b) Ideas, facts knowledge, wisdom

    c) Data, information, facts, wisdom

    d) Data, information, knowledge, wisdom

Question 4

Which activity in Service Asset and Configuration Management would help to ascertain whether the recorded Configuration Items conform to the physical environment?

    a) Control

    b) Verification and audit

    c) Identification

    d) Status accounting

Question 5

After a Change has been implemented, an evaluation is performed. What is this evaluation called?

    a) Forward Schedule of Changes (FSC)

    b) Post Implementation Review (PIR)

    c) Service Improvement Programme (SIP)

    d) Service Level Requirement (SLR)

Question 6

Which of the following is not change type?

    a) Standard change

    b) Normal change

    c) Quick change

    d) Emergency change

Question 7

Which process is responsible for maintaining software items in the Definitive Media Library (DML)?

    a) Release and Deployment Management

    b) Service Asset and Configuration Management

    c) Service validation and testing

    d) Change Management

Question 8

Which process or function is responsible for communicating the Change Schedule to the users?

    a) Change Management

    b) Service Desk

    c) Release and Deployment Management

    d) Service Level Management

Question 9

Which of the following best describes a baseline?

    a) Used as a reference point for later comparison

    b) The starting point of any project

    c) The end point of any project

    d) A rollback procedure

Question 10

The main objective of Change Management is to?

    a) Ensure that any changes are approved and recorded

    b) Ensure that standardised methods and procedures are used for controlled handling of all changes

    c) Ensure that any change requests are managed through the CAB

    d) Ensure that the CAB takes responsibility for all change implementation

7 Service Operation

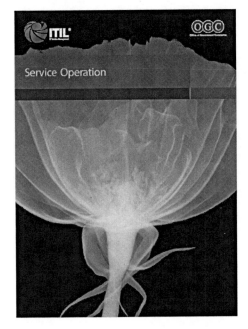

Figure 7.A – Service Operation

The Service Operation lifecycle phase is primarily focused on the management of IT Services that ensures effectiveness and efficiency in delivery and support.

Successful Service Operation requires coordination and execution of the activities and processes required to deliver and manage services at agreed levels to business users and customers. Service Operation is also responsible for ongoing management of the technology that is used to deliver and support services.

One of Service Operation's key roles is dealing with the conflict between maintaining the status quo, adapting to the changing business and technological environments and achieving a balance between conflicting sets of priorities.

7.1 Objectives

The primary objective of Service Operation is to enable effectiveness and efficiency in delivery and support of IT services.

Strategic objectives are ultimately realized through Service Operations, therefore making it a critical capability. This lifecycle phase provides guidance on:

- How to provide stability in Service Operations, allowing for changes in design, scale, scope and service levels

- Service Operation process guidelines, methods and tools for use in two major control perspectives; reactive and proactive. Managers and practitioners are provided with knowledge allowing them to make better decisions in areas such as managing the availability of services, controlling demand, optimizing capacity utilization, scheduling of operations and fixing problems

- Supporting operations through new models and architectures such as shared services, utility computing, web services and mobile commerce.

©The Art of Service

7.2 Major Concepts

Achieving the Balance

Service Operation is more than just a repetitive execution of a standard set of procedures or activities, this phase works in an ever-changing environment. One of Service Operation's key roles is dealing with the conflict between maintaining the status quo, adapting to the changing business and technological environments and achieving a balance between conflicting sets of priorities.

Figure 7.B – Achieving balance in Service Operation

Internal IT View:		External Business View:
Focuses on the way in which IT components and systems are managed to deliver the services. An organization here is out of balance and is in danger of not meeting business requirements.	VS	Focuses on the way in which services are experienced by users and customers. An organization has business focus, but tends to under-deliver on promises to the business.
Stability:		**Responsiveness:**
No matter how good the functionality is of an IT service or how well it has been designed, it will be worth far less if the service components are not available or if they perform inconsistently. Service Operation has to ensure that the IT infrastructure is stable and available as required. However an extreme focus on stability means that IT is in danger of ignoring changing business requirements	VS	Service Operation must recognize that the business and IT requirements change. When there is an extreme focus on responsiveness IT may tend to overspend on change and also decrease the stability of the infrastructure.

Cost of Service:	VS	Quality of Service:
An organization with an extreme focus on cost is out of balance and is in danger of losing service quality because of heavy cost cutting. The loss of service quality leads to a loss of customers, which in turn leads to further cost cutting as the negative cycle continues.	VS	An organization with an extreme focus on quality has happy customers but may tend to overspend to deliver higher levels of service than are strictly necessary, resulting in higher costs and effort required. The goal should be to consistently deliver the agreed level of IT service to customer and users, while at the same time keeping costs and resource utilization at an optimal level.
Reactive:	VS	**Proactive:**
An organization that is extremely reactive is not able to effectively support the business strategy. Unfortunately a lot of organizations focus on reactive management as the sole means to ensure services are highly consistent and stable, actively discouraging proactive behavior from staff. The worst aspect of this approach is that discouraging effort investment in proactive Service Management can ultimately increase the effort and cost of reactive activities and further risk stability and consistency in services.	VS	An extremely proactive organization tends to fix services that are not broken, or introduce services that are not yet needed, resulting in higher levels of change, costs and effort. This also comes at a cost of stability to the infrastructure and quality of service already being delivered.

7.3 Service Operation Functions

Functions refer to the people (or roles) and automated measures that execute a defined process, an activity or combination of both. The functions within Service Operation are needed to manage the 'steady state' operation IT environment. Just like in sports where each player will have a specific role to play in the overall team strategy, IT Functions define the different roles and responsibilities required for the overall Service Delivery and Support of IT Services.

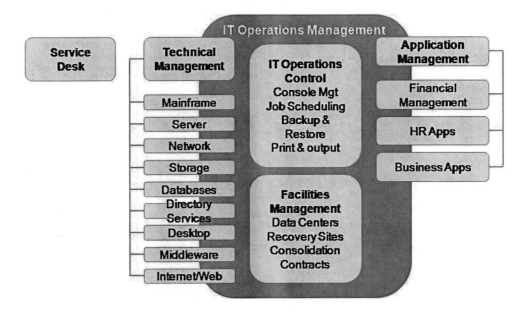

Figure 7.C – The ITIL® Functions from Service Operation

Note: These are logical functions and do not necessarily have to be performed by equivalent organizational structure. This means that Technical and Application Management can be organized in any combination and into any number of departments. The lower groupings (e.g. Mainframe, Server) are examples of activities performed by Technical Management and are not a suggested organizational structure.

7.3.1 The Service Desk

7.3.1.1 Goal and objectives

The primary goal of the Service Desk is to support the agreed IT service provision by ensuring the accessibility and availability of the IT-organization and by performing various supporting activities. Other objectives include:

- To act as a single point of contact for all user incidents, requests and general communication
- To restore 'normal service operation' as quickly as possible in the case of disruption
- To improve user awareness of IT issues and to promote appropriate use of IT services and resources
- To assist other the other IT functions by managing user communication and escalating incidents and requests using defined procedures.

7.3.1.2 Service Desk organizational structures

Many factors will influence the way in which a Service Desk function will be physically structured, such as the location, languages and cultures of end users, diversity in services and technology supported and the objectives governing the implementation of the Service Desk such as improved satisfaction or reduced operating costs.

The following are some of the main options chosen when implementing a Service Desk function:

Local Service Desk

A local Service Desk structure is where the Service Desk is co-located within or physically close to the user community it serves. This may aid in communication and give the Service Desk a visible presence which some users may like. It may however be inefficient and expensive to have multiple Service Desks operating.

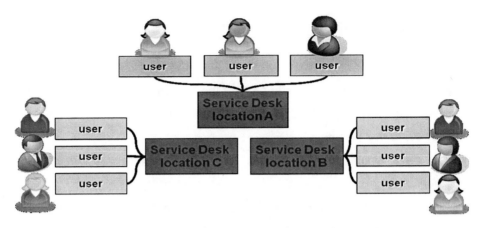

Figure 7.D – The local Service Desk structure

Benefits of a Local Service Desk structure	Disadvantages of a Local Service Desk structure
• Local and specific user knowledge • Ability to effectively communicate with multiple languages • Appropriate cultural knowledge • Visible (and physical) presence of the Service Desk	• Higher costs for replicated infrastructure and more staff involved • Less knowledge transfer, each Service Desk may spend time rediscovering knowledge • Inconsistency in service levels and reporting • Service Desks may be focused on local issues.

Centralized Service Desk

A centralized structure uses a Service Desk in a single location (or smaller number of locations), although some local presence may remain to handle physical support requirements such as deploying, moving and disposing of user workstations. This could be more efficient, enabling less staff to manage a higher volume of calls, with greater visibility of repeat incidents and requests.

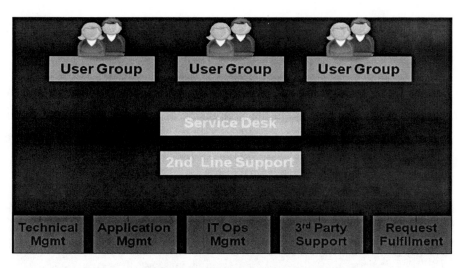

Figure 7.E – The centralized Service Desk structure

Benefits of a centralized Service Desk structure	Disadvantages of a centralized Service Desk structure
• Reduced operational costs • Improved usage of available resources • Consistency of call handling • Improved ability for knowledge sharing • Simplicity for users (call one number) to contact the Service Desk	• Potentially higher costs and challenges in handling 24x7 environment or different time zone • Lack of local knowledge • Possible gaps in language and culture • Higher risk (single point of failure), in case of power loss or other physical threat.

Virtual Service Desk

A Virtual Service Desk, through the use of technology, particularly the Internet and the use of corporate support tools, can give users the impression of a single, centralized Service Desk when in fact the personnel may be spread or located in any number of geographical or structural locations.

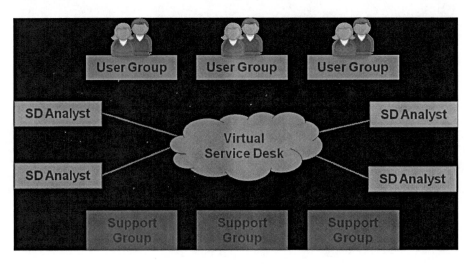

Figure 7.F – A virtual Service Desk structure

Benefits of a virtual Service Desk structure	Disadvantages of a virtual Service Desk structure
• Support for global organizations • 24x7 support in multiple time zones • Reduced operational costs • Improved usage of available resources • Effective matching of appropriate staff for different types of calls	• Initial cost of implementation, requiring diverse and effective voice technology • Lack in the consistency of service and reporting • Less effective for monitoring actions of staff • Staff may feel disconnected from other Service Desk staff.

Follow the Sun

Some global or international organizations will combine two or more of their geographically dispersed Service Desks to provide 24-hour follow-the-sun service.

Figure 7.G – A 'Follow the Sun' Service Desk structure

Benefits of a 'Follow the Sun' Service Desk structure	Disadvantages of a 'Follow the Sun' Service Desk structure
• Support for global organizations • 24x7 support in multiple time zones • Improved quality of service • Improved customer/user satisfaction • Effective knowledge sharing and high level visibility of distributed infrastructure	• Typically higher operating costs • Cost of required technology • Challenges in using single language for multiple regions when recording knowledge, workarounds, Known Errors etc.

©The Art of Service

7.3.1.3 Skills

Due to the role played by the Service Desk, staff members need to have (or have the ability to develop):

- Communication Skills
- Technical Skills
- Business Understanding.

The most important of these three is communication skills, as the primary role of the Service Desk is to provide a Single Point of Contact between the end-users and the IT organization. Because of this, they will need to be able to deal effectively with a wide range of people and situations.

7.3.1.4 Staff Retention

To ensure a balanced mix of experienced and newer staff, Service Desk Managers should use a number of methods and incentives to retain quality staff and to avoid disruption and inconsistency in the quality of support offered.

Some ways in which this can be done include:

- Recognition of staff achievements contributing to service quality
- Rotation of staff onto other activities (projects, second-line support etc.)
- Team building exercises and celebrations
- Promote the Service Desk as a potential stepping stone for staff to move into other more technical or supervisory roles (after defined time periods and skills achieved).

7.3.1.5 Self help

Many organizations find it beneficial to offer "self help" capabilities to their users. The technology should therefore support this capability, with the web front-end allowing web pages offering a menu-driven range of self help and service requests – with a direct interface into the back-end process-handling software. This reduces the amount of calls into the Service Desk and is often used as a source for improvements to efficiency. An example of this is the ability for a customer to track online the status of their parcels when shipped through a major courier company.

Aside from this, the Service Desk will use many different tools, systems and other technology components in order to provide effective and efficient support to end-user calls and requests. To enable this, typical technology components utilized include:

- Computerized service desk systems
- Voice services (adv. menu systems, voicemail, SMS)
- Web and email (access, notification, updates)
- Systems that contain linkages to SLAs, CMDB
- Access to availability monitoring tools
- Self help for customers using technology.

7.3.1.6 Service Desk Metrics

To evaluate the true performance of the Service Desk, a balanced range of metrics should be established and reviewed at regular intervals. Especially dangerous is the tendency to focus on "average call time" or "number of calls answered" metrics, which can mask underlying issues with the quality of support provided.

Some of the typical metrics reviewed when monitoring the performance of the Service Desk include:

- The number of calls to Service Desk (broken down by type and work period)
- First-line resolution rate
- Average Service Desk cost of handling any incident or request
- Number of knowledgebase articles created
- Number or percentage of SLA breaches
- Call resolution time
- Customer satisfaction (surveys)
- Use of self help (where exists).

7.3.1.7 Outsourcing the Service Desk

Although fairly common, there are potential risks that can be introduced when outsourcing an organization's Service Desk. When reviewing the potential for this to occur, Service Managers should consider the following items when developing contracts to reduce these risks:

- Use of your own Service Management tool, not theirs
- Retain ownership of data
- Ability to maintain required staffing levels
- Agreements on reporting and monitoring needs
- Proven up to date procedures
- Agreed and understood support needs
- Engage contract specialists for assistance.

7.3.2 Technical Management

7.3.2.1 Goal and objectives

The Technical Management function's primary goal is to plan, implement and maintain a stable technical infrastructure that supports the organization's business processes.

This is achieved through:
- Well designed, highly resilient, cost effective technical architectures
- The use of adequate technical skills to maintain the technical infrastructure in optimum condition
- Swift use of technical skills to speedily diagnose and resolve any technical failures that do occur.

One or more technical support teams or departments will be needed to provide Technical Management and support for the IT Infrastructure.

In all but the smallest organizations where a single combined team or department may suffice, separate teams or departments will be needed for each type of infrastructure being used. In many organizations the Technical Management (TM) departments are also responsible for the daily operation of a subset of the IT Infrastructure.

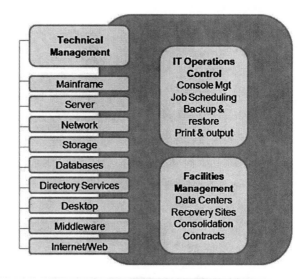

Figure 7.H – Technical Management

In many organizations, the actual role played by IT Operations Management is carried out by either Technical or Application Management.

7.3.2.2 Roles and Responsibilities

- Custodian of technical knowledge and expertise related to managing the IT Infrastructure. Provides detailed technical skills and resources needed to support the ongoing operation of the IT Infrastructure.

- Plays an important role in providing the actual resources to support the IT Service Management lifecycle. Ensures resources are effectively trained and deployed to design, build, transition, operate and improve the technology to deliver and support IT Services.

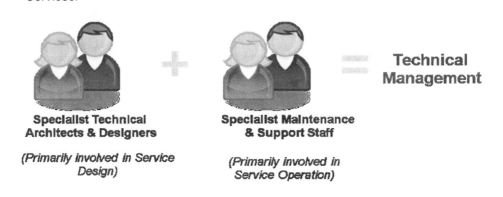

Specialist Technical Architects & Designers

(Primarily involved in Service Design)

Specialist Maintenance & Support Staff

(Primarily involved in Service Operation)

Technical Management

Figure 7.1 – Staff making up the Technical Management Function

To enable quality knowledge sharing and continual improvement of services, technology, processes and other capabilities, Technical Management staff should develop effective communication channels and meet regularly to discuss issues or potential ideas. History demonstrates that quality design requires involvement from those who will be supporting the product/service, as does quality support require involvement from the designers in turn.

7.3.3 IT Operations Management

7.3.3.1 Goal and objectives

The primary goal of IT Operations Management is to perform the IT organization's day to day operational activities using repeatable and consistent actions. Some of the objectives include:

- Maintenance of the 'status quo' to achieve stability of the organization's day to day processes and activities
- Regular scrutiny and improvements to achieve improved service at reduced costs, whilst maintaining stability
- Swift application of operational skills to diagnose and resolve any IT operations failures that occur.

In some organizations this is a single, centralized department, while in others some activities and staff are centralized and some are provided by distributed and specialized departments.

In many cases, the role of IT Operations Management is actually performed by the Technical and Application Management functions where required.

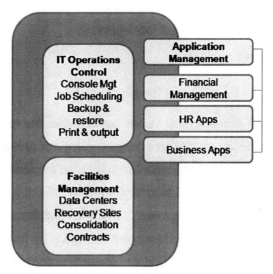

Figure 7.1 – IT Operations Management

7.3.3.2 IT Operations Control

One role played by IT Operations Management is that of Operations Control. This role is concerned with the execution and monitoring of the operational activities and events in the IT infrastructure (possibly using an Operations/Network Bridge). In addition to the routine tasks to be performed in accordance with the design specifications of the IT infrastructure, Operations Control is also responsible for the following:

- Monitoring and Control
- Console Management
- Job Scheduling
- Backup and restores
- Print and Output Management.

7.3.3.3 Facilities Management

Facilities Management refers to the role responsible for management of all physical IT environments, usually data centers, computer rooms and recovery sites. In some organizations many physical components have been outsourced and Facilities Management may include the management of the outsourcing contracts. For any organization this is a very important element of IT Service Management, and will contribute to the ability to provide a safe working environment. Facilities Management should be involved in any large scale and project planning to provide advice regarding any physical accommodation of staff or infrastructure required.

7.3.4 Application Management

7.3.4.1 Goal and objectives

Application Management's primary goal is to develop, maintain and support quality applications that enhance the organization's business processes. This goal is achieved through:

- Applications that are well designed, interface with existing architectures, are resilient and cost-effective
- Ensuring the functionality and performance requirements of the business are delivered in optimal fashion
- The use of technical skills to maintain availability of applications
- Swift response to diagnose and resolve any disruptions that occur.

Application Management is usually divided into departments based on the application portfolio of the organization allowing easier specialization and more focused support.

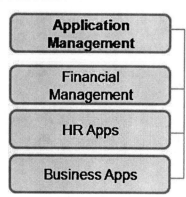

Figure 7.J –
Application Management

7.3.4.2 Roles and Responsibilities

- Managing Applications throughout their lifecycle
- Supports and maintains operational applications, and plays an important role in design, testing and improvement of applications that form part of IT Services
- Support the organization's business processes by helping to identify functional and manageability requirements for application software
- Assisting in the decision whether to build or buy an application
- Assist in the design and/or deployment of those applications
- Provide ongoing support and improvement of those applications
- Identify skills required to support the applications.

7.3.4.3 Application Management Lifecycle

Application Development processes should be implemented as part of a coordinated approach to IT Service Management, although in many cases this fails to happen. When the development of applications is not integrated with the rest of ITSM, it often leads to a breakdown in communication channels between developers and support staff, and ultimately releasing applications that are not optimal in supporting business processes.

Application Development and Operations are part of the same overall lifecycle and both should be involved at all stages, although their level of involvement will vary depending on the stage of the lifecycle.

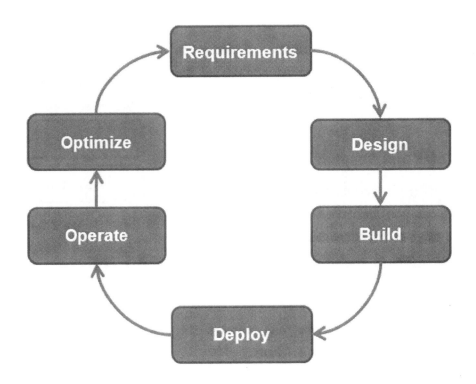

Figure 7.J: The Application Management Lifecycle

© Crown Copyright 2007 Reproduced under license from OGC

7.4 Service Operation Processes

The goal of Service Operation, as previously mentioned, is to enable effectiveness and efficiency in delivery and support of IT services. The processes that support this goal are:

- Event Management
- Incident Management
- Problem Management
- Request Fulfillment
- Access Management.

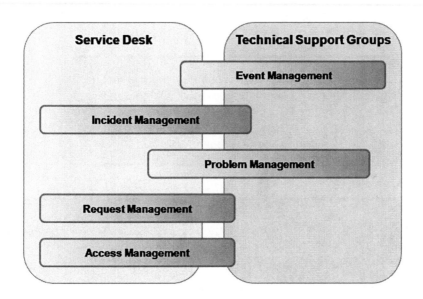

Figure 7.K – Where the Service Operation Processes get carried out

The figure above demonstrates how much responsibility the Service Desk and the Technical Support Groups (Technical, IT Operations and Application Management functions) have in the Service Operation Processes. Incident Management, Request Fulfillment and Access Management are primarily carried out by the Service Desk, with Event Management and Problem Management as primarily 'back-of-house' processes.

7.4.1 Event Management

7.4.1.1 Goal and objectives

The goal of Event Management is to provide the capability to detect events, make sense of them and determine the appropriate control action. Event Management is therefore the basis for Operational Monitoring and Control.

Event Management should be utilized to detect and communicate operational information as well as warnings and exceptions, so that input can be provided for reporting the service achievements and quality levels provided. It may be used for automating routine activities such as backups and batch processing, or dynamic roles for balancing demand for services across multiple infrastructure items/sources to improve performance.

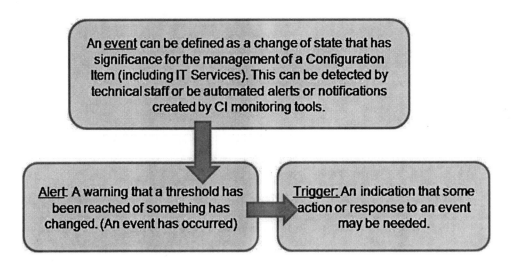

An <u>event</u> can be defined as a change of state that has significance for the management of a Configuration Item (including IT Services). This can be detected by technical staff or be automated alerts or notifications created by CI monitoring tools.

<u>Alert</u>: A warning that a threshold has been reached of something has changed. (An event has occurred)

<u>Trigger:</u> An indication that some action or response to an event may be needed.

There are many different types of events, for example:

- Informational events that signify regular operation *(e.g. A scheduled backup occurred successfully)*
- Exception events *(e.g. A scheduled backup failed)*
- Warning events that signify unusual but not exceptional operation. These are an indication that the situation may require closer monitoring *(e.g. No backup initiated within last 72 hours)*.

7.4.1.2 Activities

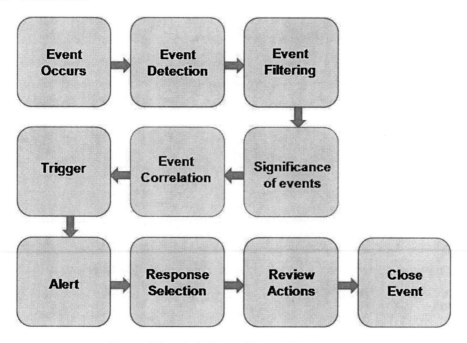

Figure 7.L – Activities of Event Management

Note: In most organizations' IT infrastructure there would be a significant amount of events occurring every day, which may impact on the way in which events are correlated and provide triggers indicating if or when a response is needed.

7.4.1.3 Scope

Event Management can be applied to any aspect of Service Management that needs to be controlled and which can be automated. These include:

- CIs - to provide visibility of functioning and failing components, or to understand when other changes have occurred in the infrastructure
- Environmental conditions – such as increases in the temperature of servers and facilities
- Software license monitoring – used to maintain optimum licensing utilization
- Security – to perform security checks and to detect exceptions or intrusions
- Normal activity – such as tracking the activity and performance of an IT service.

It is important to note the difference between monitoring and Event Management. While the two areas are related, Event Management focuses on the generation and detection of notifications about the status of the IT infrastructure and services. Monitoring on the other hand has a broader scope, which will include monitoring CIs that do not generate events or alerts. So when implementing Event Management, consider what monitoring activities and techniques should be interfaced to generate alerts and notifications that will provide value to the IT groups and wider organization.

7.4.1.4 Event Correlation

When the significance has been determined, correlation is used to compare the event with a set of criteria and rules in a specific order. The rules may have either a technical or business focus, but the underlying reason for correlation is to determine the level and type of business impact of the event.

A 'Correlation Engine' should be programmed during the Service Design phase, utilizing the guidelines provided by Service Operation. Correlation Engines will use a number of factors to make decisions, including:

- The categorization of the event
- The number of similar events have occurred
- Number of CIs generating similar events
- Whether the event indicates an exception
- A comparison against defined threshold levels (e.g. utilization levels)
- Whether further information is required to investigate further.

These factors should also be used to set a priority level for the event, in order to define the appropriate level of response from the operations group.

7.4.1.5 Event Management Interfaces

Event Management should be developed over time to any service management process that requires monitoring and control. While initially the focus will be on providing the foundation for service operation with input to Incident and Problem Management, other possible interfaces that are appropriate include:

- Configuration Management, with events providing information on the current (real-time) and historical status of CIs
- Service Design processes such as Information Security, Capacity and Availability Management. Where thresholds have been set in the design of a service and associated components, Event Management should be utilized to generate events and response actions
- Service Level Management, where Event Management can enhance the capabilities to safeguard SLAs and reduce the business impact of any failures as soon as possible.

7.4.2 Incident Management

Incident Management has developed over time to become one of the most visible and mature ITIL processes for any organization, largely driven by the need to reduce the business impact of disruptions to IT services. While any effective implementation does balance the efforts towards the various phases of the Service Lifecycle, as Incident Management can be easily demonstrated to have a business benefit, it typically receives more attention and funding than other areas of service management. This section will explain the activities and techniques that represent best practices for Incident Management.

7.4.2.1 Goal and objectives

The goal of Incident Management is *to restore normal service operation as quickly as possible* and minimize the adverse impact on business operations, thus ensuring that the best possible levels of service quality and availability are maintained.

Normal service operation is defined as operating within the agreed Service Level Agreement (SLA) limits.

What is the difference between Incident Management and Problem Management?

If our garden had weeds, how would we address the situation?

Incident Management: Use techniques that address the symptoms but still allow the weeds to grow back (e.g. Pull them out, mow over them, use a hedge-trimmer, and buy a goat)

Problem Management: Use techniques that address the root-cause of the symptoms, so that weeds will no longer grow (e.g. Use poison, dig roots out, re-lawn, concrete over etc.)

Incident Management is not concerned with the root cause; it is instead focused on addressing the symptoms as quickly as possible.

7.4.2.2 Scope

Incident Management can be utilized to manage any event which disrupts, or has the potential to disrupt an IT service and associated business processes. Careful distinction needs to be made between the role of Event Management and Incident Management, as only events that indicate exception to normal service operation and are determined by the Event Correlation engine to be significant are escalated to Incident Management. This means that incident records may be generated as a result of:

- End users calling the Service Desk to notify of a disruption to their normal use of IT services

- Events representing an exception that are resolved using automated means, with an associated incident record also being generated for informational purposes
- An IT staff member noticing that a component of the IT infrastructure is behaving abnormally, despite no current impact on the end user community
- An end user logging an incident using self help means, which is then resolved by IT operations staff
- An external supplier observes that a portion of the IT infrastructure under their control is experiencing issues, and logs an incident ticket via email.

While the process of Request Fulfillment does typically operate in a similar fashion to Incident Management, a service request does not involve any (potential) disruption to an IT service.

7.4.2.3 Incident Models

Incident Models provide a pre-defined set of steps and procedures that should be used to manage previously seen and documented incidents. They are used to help provide efficient resolution to the most frequently occurring (80/20 rule) or specialized incidents. Incident Models should define:

- The steps that should be taken to handle the incident
- The chronological order these steps should be taken in, with any dependencies or co-processing defined
- Responsibilities, who should do what
- Timescales and thresholds for completion of actions
- Escalation procedures, who should be contacted and when
- Any necessary evidence-preservation activities.

Any service management tools that are used for Event and Incident Management should be utilized with the defined incident models that can automate the handling, management and escalation of the process.

Specialized incidents include those which need routing to particular groups or ITIL processes. An example of this is for capacity related incidents, in which the model would define what impact reduction measures could be performed before routing the incident to Capacity Management.

7.4.2.4 Major incidents

For those incidents that result in significant or organization-wide business impact, planning needs to consider how separate procedures should be used with shorter timescales and greater urgency to provide appropriate response and resolution. The first requirement is to define what constitutes a major incident for the organization and customers, with reference to the incident prioritization mechanisms that are used.

The key role of separate major incident procedures is to establish a fast and coordinated response that can manage and resolve the issues at hand. This may require the establishment of a team with the immediate focus of resolving the incident and reducing the associated business impact. The Service Desk maintains responsibility throughout the process so that users are kept fully informed of the incident status and progress for resolution.

Problem Management will typically be involved when major incidents occur, though the focus is not the resolution of the incident. Instead Problem Management seeks to identify the root cause of the incident, how this can be removed and if there are any other areas of the infrastructure where this could occur (e.g. replicated infrastructure across multiple locations).

7.4.2.5 Activities

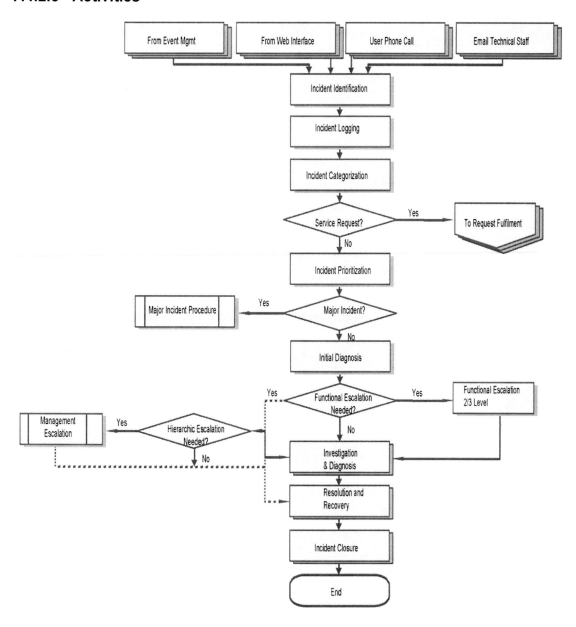

Figure 7.M: – Typical activities for Incident Management

© Crown Copyright 2007 Reproduced under license from OGC

Overview of steps

1. Incident identification
2. Incident logging
3. Incident categorization
4. Incident prioritization
5. Initial diagnosis
6. Incident escalation
7. Investigation and diagnosis
8. Resolution and recovery
9. Incident closure.

1. Incident identification

The implementation of Incident Management should consider the range of sources where incidents can be identified. These typically include:

- Customers and end users
- External customers (of the business)
- IT staff members
- Automated mechanisms, including those governed by Event Management
- External suppliers.

2. Incident logging

All incidents, regardless of source, must be recorded with a unique reference number and be date/time stamped. While this can be easily managed for automated mechanisms, positive behaviors need to be developed for IT staff and end users to ensure the consistent recording of identified incidents. It may also be necessary to record more than one incident for any given call/discussion so that a historical record is kept and that time/work tracking can be performed.

3. Incident categorization

During the initial logging of the incident, a category is assigned so that the exact type of incident is recorded. This information is important to allow effective escalation, trend analysis of incidents and future infrastructure improvements. Multi-level categorization is typically used for Incident Management, where the service management tool is populated with up to three of four levels of category details.

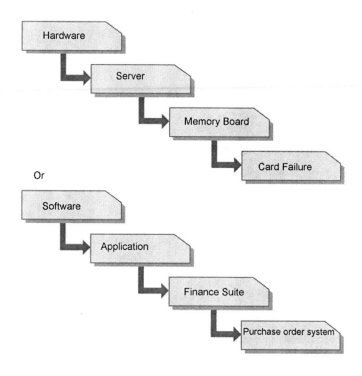

Figure 7.N: Multi-level incident categorization
© *Crown Copyright 2007 Reproduced under license from OGC*

4. Incident prioritization

An agreed prioritization matrix should be used to determine the appropriate timescales and effort applied for response and resolution to identified incidents. The general formula by which to calculate incident priority is:

IMPACT + URGENCY = PRIORITY

- **Impact:** Degree to which the **user/business** is affected by the incident(s)
- **Urgency:** Degree to which the **resolution** of the incident can be delayed

For following factors are usually taken into account for determining the impact of an incident:
- The number of users being affected
    - (e.g. single user, multiple users, entire business unit, organization wide)
- Possible risk of injury or death
- The number of services affected
- The level of financial loss
- Effect on credibility and reputation of business
- Regulatory or legislative breaches.

Urgency is calculated by assessing when the potential impact of the incident will be felt. In some cases the incident resolution can be delayed when the disruption to an IT service (e.g. payroll) has not yet affected business operations (but will if the service is not available in three days time).

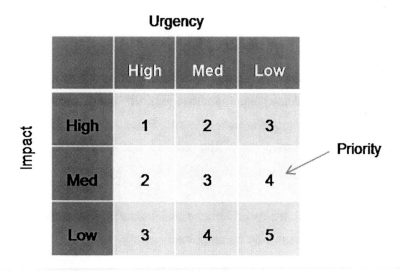

Figure 7.O: Example incident prioritization matrix

The prioritization matrix above would be accompanied by agreed timelines for resolution.

E.g.

Priority 1 =	Critical	=	1 hour target resolution time
Priority 2 =	High	=	8 hours
Priority 3 =	Medium	=	24 hours
Priority 4 =	Low	=	48 hours.

5. Initial diagnosis

For calls forwarded to the Service Desk, the staff member will use pre-defined questioning techniques to assist in the collection of useful information for the incident record. At this point the Service Desk analyst can begin to provide some initial support by referencing known errors and simple diagnostic tools. Where possible the incident will be resolved using these sources of information, closing the incident after verifying the resolution was successful.

For incidents that can't be resolved at this stage and the user is still on the phone, the Service Desk analyst should inform the user of the next steps that will be taken, give the unique incident reference number and confirm user contact details for follow-ups.

6. Incident escalation

If the Service Desk analyst requires assistance from other groups due to an inability to resolve the incident or because of specialized circumstances (e.g. VIP user), escalation will be utilized to transfer the incident to the appropriate party or group. Rules for escalation should be defined when implementing Incident Management and agreed upon by all involved groups and stakeholders.

The two forms of escalation that are typically used are functional (horizontal) and hierarchical (vertical) escalation. Escalations can also be combined.

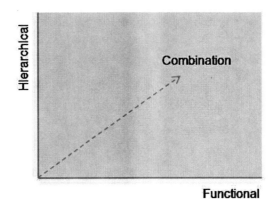

Figure 7.P: Example incident prioritization matrix

Functional:

- Based on *knowledge or expertise*
- Also known as "Horizontal Escalation", through level 1, 2, and 3 support.

Hierarchical:

- For corrective actions by authorized *line management*
- Also known as "Vertical Escalation"
- When resolution of an incident will not be in time or satisfactory.

7. Investigation and diagnosis

The incident investigation is likely to include such actions as:

- Establishing exactly what has gone wrong or what is being sought by the user
- Understanding the chronological order of events
- Confirming the full impact of the incident, including the number and range of users affected
- Identifying any events that could have triggered the incident
- Knowledge searches looking for previous occurrences by searching previous Incident/Problem Records and/or Known/Error databases etc.
- Seeking knowledge from system developers as to possible guidance for resolution.

8. Resolution and recovery

When a potential resolution has been identified, it should be applied and tested in a controlled manner. The specific requirements for performing this will vary depending on the elements required for resolution, but could involve:

- Guiding the user to perform specific actions on their own equipment
- Specialist support groups performing specific actions on the infrastructure (such as rebooting a server)
- External suppliers performing updates on their infrastructure in order to resolve the incident
- The Service Desk or other specialist staff controlling a user's desktop remotely in order to resolve the incident.

9. Incident closure

Depending on the nature of the incident (level of impact, users affected etc.), the Service Desk may be required to call the affected users and confirm that the users are satisfied that the resolution was successful and that the incident can be closed. For other incidents, closure mechanisms may be automated and communicated via email. Closure mechanisms, whether automated or manual, should also check for the following:

- Closure categorization, with comparison to the initial categorization to ensure accurate historical tracking
- User satisfaction survey, usually be email or web-forms for an agreed percentage of random incidents
- Incident documentation, ensuring all required fields are completed satisfactorily
- Potential problem identification, assisting Problem Management in the decision whether any preventative action is necessary to avoid this in the future.

When the requirements for incident documentation are complete, the incident should be closed via agreed methods.

7.4.2.6 Roles and Responsibilities

Incident Manager:

- Drive effectiveness and efficiency of process
- Manage incident management team
- Ensure SLA targets for Incident resolution are met.

Skills: Analytical, technical, business understanding, communication, calm under pressure.

Service Desk:

- Log/record Incidents
- Incident classification and categorization
- Provide initial support
- Match to existing Incident or Problem records
- Manage communication with end users.

1st, 2nd, 3rd line support groups (including Technical and Application Management):

- Incident classification
- Investigation and resolution of Incidents

7.4.2.7 Incident Management Metrics

Just like any other ITIL® process, a balanced range of metrics must be used to demonstrate effectiveness and efficiency of the Incident Management process, including:

- Total number of incidents
- Percentage of Incidents handled within agreed response time (Incident response-time targets may be specified in SLAs, for example, by impact code)
- Average cost per Incident
- Percentage of Incidents closed by the Service Desk without reference to other levels of support
- Number and percentage of Incidents resolved remotely, without the need for a physical visit.

7.4.2.8 Challenges affecting Incident Management

- Are all calls registered? Are they assigned a unique number?
- Which priority codes do we use and how is the priority determined?
- Organization of the 1st line support group (Service Desk)
- Organization of the 2nd line, which may be from disparate support groups
- What percentage of "closed on first call" is possible through Incident Management?

©The Art of Service

7.4.3 Problem Management

7.4.3.1 Goal and objectives

Problem Management is responsible for managing lifecycle of all problems. The primary objectives of Problem Management are:

- To prevent problems and resulting incidents from happening
- To eliminate recurring incidents
- To minimize the impact of incidents that cannot be prevented.

7.4.3.2 Scope

Clear distinction should be made between the purpose, scope and activities of Problem Management and those of Incident Management. In many cases, staff may not clearly understand the distinction, and as a result not utilize their efforts in the most effective and efficient manner.

For most implementations of Problem Management the scope includes:
- The activities required to diagnose the root cause of incidents and to determine the resolution to those problems
- Activities that ensure that the resolution is implemented through the appropriate control procedures, usually through interfaces with Change Management and Release and Deployment Management
- Proactive activities that eliminate errors in the infrastructure before they result in incidents and impact on the business and end users.

Defined as two major processes:
- Reactive Problem Management
- Proactive Problem Management **

** Initiated in Service Operation but generally driven as part of Continual Service Improvement.

Remember the weeding analogy used for Incident Management? Problem Management seeks to identify and remove the root-cause of Incidents in the IT Infrastructure.

Terminology	Explanations
Problem:	**Unknown** underlying cause of one or more Incidents (The investigation)
Known Error:	**Known** underlying cause. Successful diagnosis of the root cause of a Problem, and workaround or permanent solution has been identified
KEDB:	Known Error Database, where Known Errors and their documented workarounds are maintained. This database is owned by Problem Management.
Workaround:	The pre-defined and documented technique used to restore normal service operation for the user. A workaround is NOT a permanent (structural) solution, and only addresses the symptoms of errors. These workarounds are stored in the KEDB (or Service Knowledge Management System).

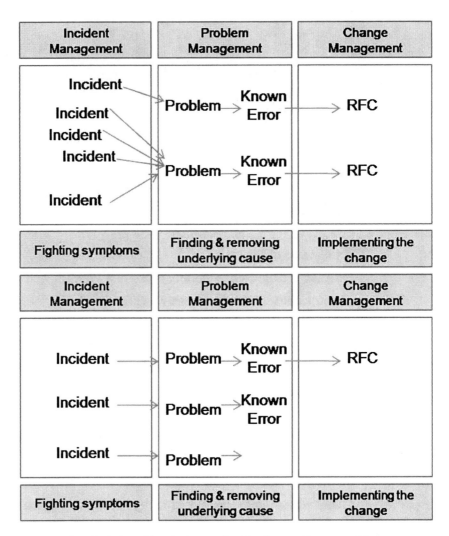

Figure 7.Q – Relationships between incidents, problems and known errors

As shown above, Problems are identified and corrected in multiple ways. For most organizations, the primary benefit of Problem Management is demonstrated in the "Many to One" relationship between Incidents and Problems. This enables an IT Service Provider to resolve many Incidents in an efficient manner by correcting the underlying root-cause. Change Management is still required so that the actions being performed to correct and remove the error are done so in a controlled and efficient manner.

Why do some Problems not get diagnosed?

- Because the root cause is not always found.

Why do some Known Errors not get fixed?

- Because we may decide that the costs exceed the benefits of fixing the error; or
- Because it may be fixed in an upcoming patch from development teams or suppliers.

7.4.3.3 Two Sub-Processes of Problem Management

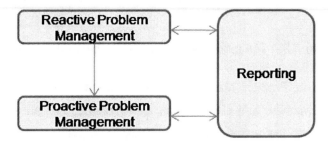

Figure 7.R – The two sub-processes of Problem Management

The activities of Problem Management are carried out within the Proactive and Reactive Problem Management. The main goal of Proactive Problem Management is to identify errors that might otherwise be missed. Proactive Problem Management analyzes Incident Records, and uses data collected by other IT Service Management processes and external sources to identify trends or significant problems.

7.4.3.4 Reactive Problem Management

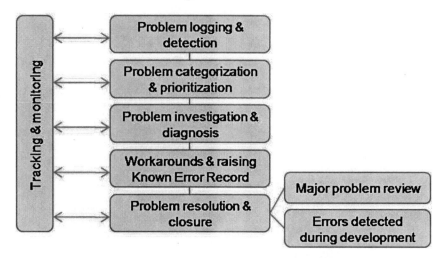

Figure 7.S – The activities of Reactive Problem Management

The activities of Reactive Problem Management are similar to those of Incident Management for the logging, categorization and classification for Problems. The subsequent activities are different as this is where the actual root-cause analysis is performed and the Known Error corrected.

Overview of Reactive Problem Management activities:

1. Problem detection
2. Problem logging
3. Problem categorization
4. Problem investigation and diagnosis
5. Workarounds (attached to the Problem or Known Error record)
6. Raising a Known Error record
7. Problem resolution
8. Problem closure
9. Major Problem reviews

Major Problem Review:

After every major problem, while memories are still fresh, a review should be conducted to learn any lessons for the future. Specifically the review should examine:

- Those things that were done correctly
- Those things that were done wrong
- What could be done better in the future?
- How to prevent recurrence
- Whether there has been any third-party responsibility and whether follow-up actions are needed.

Such reviews can be used as part of training and awareness activities for staff – any lessons learned should be documented in appropriate procedures, working instructions, diagnostic scripts or Known Error Records.

7.4.3.5 Proactive Problem Management

The two main activities of Proactive Problem Management are:

Trend Analysis

- Review reports from other processes (e.g. trends in incidents, availability levels, relationships with changes and releases)
- Identify recurring Problems or training opportunities for IT staff, customers and end users.

Targeting Preventative Action

- Perform a cost-benefit analysis of all costs associated with prevention
- Target specific areas taking up the most support attention
- Coordinate preventative action with Availability and Capacity Management, focusing on vulnerable areas of the infrastructure (e.g. single points of failure, components reaching full capacity/utilization).

7.4.3.6 Roles and Responsibilities

Problem Manager

- Drive effectiveness and efficiency of process
- Manage the Problem Management team
- Liaise with customers, IT executive, IT platform managers.

Skills: Business knowledge, lateral thinker, coordination skills.

Problem Management Team (including Application and Technical Management functions)

- Reactive and proactive problem management
- Provide management reports
- Assist Incident Management.

Skills: Analytical, technical, business knowledge.

7.4.4 Request Fulfillment

7.4.4.1 Goal

Request Fulfillment is concerned with fulfilling requests from the end user community using consistent and repeatable methods. The objectives include:

- To provide a channel for users to request and receive standard services for which a pre-defined approval (from Change Management) qualification exists
- To provide information to users and customers about the availability of services and the procedure for obtaining them
- To source and deliver the components of requested standard services
- To assist with general information, complaints or comments.

7.4.4.2 Scope

The scope of Request Fulfillment is influenced heavily by the success of Change Management and what types of pre-approved changes can be effectively managed, controlled and implemented by the IT department. As part of continual improvement, the scope of Request Fulfillment should grow over time as maturity develops for Service Requests, including:

- Users and customers asking questions, providing comments and making complaints
- Users seeking changes to their access levels (utilizes Access Management)
- Users wishing to have common services and applications installed for their use (including Standard Changes).

Many elements of Request Fulfillment may be automated through the use of self help such as websites and user applications, with manual activities used where necessary to fulfill the request.

7.4.4.3 Request Models

As many service requests are frequently recurring, predefined request models should be defined that document:

- What activities are required to fulfill the request
- The roles and responsibilities involved
- Target timescales and escalation paths
- Other policies or requirements that apply.

Similar to Change Models, this will enable the IT department (and the Service Desk in particular) to have a clear definition of the appropriate types of Service Requests and repeatable actions describing how requests should be fulfilled.

7.4.4.4 Activities

1. Menu selection

Where practical, some mechanism of self help should be utilized so that users can generate Service Requests using technology that interfaces with existing Service Management tools. This might be via a website that offers users a menu-driven interface, where they can select common services and provide input details. In some instances the Fulfillment of the Service Request can be entirely automated using workflow, ERP, software deployment and other tools. For others, manual activities will be required to fulfill the request using resources from the IT department, suppliers or other parties involved in the provision of IT services.

2. Financial Approval

While the Service Request may already have approval from Change Management, there may be some form of financial approval that is required when there are financial implications (usually those above a defined dollar amount). It may be possible to agree upon fixed prices for 'standard' requests, otherwise the cost must be estimated and submitted to the user/customer for financial approval (who may in turn require their own line management/financial approval).

3. 'Other' Approval

Where there may be compliance and regulatory implications for the service request, wider business approval may be needed. These approval mechanisms should be built into the request models as appropriate. Change Management should establish that there are mechanisms in place to check for, and safeguard these conditions in order for the standard change to be qualified for preapproval.

4. Fulfillment

The tasks required for Fulfillment will vary depending on the characteristics of the service request at hand. Some requests can be fulfilled using only automated mechanisms. Others may be fulfilled by the Service Desk at the first-line, or escalated where necessary to internal or external specialist groups. To ensure compatibility, Request Fulfillment should be interfaced with existing procurement and supplier processes; however the Service Desk should maintain control and visibility for all requests regardless where it is fulfilled.

5. Closure

When the Service Request has been fulfilled, it should be referred back to the Service Desk to initiate closure. This should include some verification that the request has been satisfied using either confirmation with the end user or other automated means.

7.4.5 Access Management

7.4.5.1 Goal and objectives

Access Management's primary objective is to provide capabilities for the granting of authorized users the right to use a service while preventing access to non-authorized users. In doing so, it helps to protect the confidentiality, integrity and availability (CIA) of the organization's services, assets, facilities and information. In practice, Access Management is the operational enforcement of the policies defined by Information Security Management.

7.4.5.2 Relationship with other Processes

Access Management ensures that users are given the right to use a service, but it does not ensure that this access is available at all agreed times – this is provided by Availability Management. As described above, the process is often centrally coordinated by the Service Desk (being the single point of contact with the end user community), but can involve the Technical and Application Management functions. Where access is controlled by external suppliers, interfaces need to be developed to coordinate requests for/modifications to access levels.

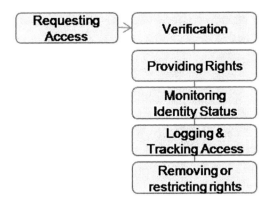

Figure 7.T – Access Management Activities

Figure 7.T demonstrates the lifecycle for managing access to services, information and facilities. In many implementations, these activities relate to the lifecycle of a user as they join the organization, change roles (possibly many times) and finally leave the organization. There should be integration with existing business processes for human resources so that access levels can be continually checked for accuracy against defined job roles.

7.4.5.3 Triggers and Interfaces

The execution of Access Management activities is normally triggered by:

- Service Requests, taken by the Service Desk or submitted using automated and self help mechanisms
- Requests from Human Resources personnel
- Direct requests from department managers
- Request for Changes (RFCs) involving modification of access rights
- Requests for enabling restricted access to contractors and external suppliers.

Some of the key interfaces that need to be maintained within the Service Lifecycle are:

- **Service Design**
  - Information Security Management, in the development and renewal of security policies, guidelines and procedures, which are then executed by Access Management
  - Availability Management, in the design of security systems and infrastructure
- **Service Transition**
  - Change Management, which should coordinate changes to processes and any groups and roles defined for Access Management
  - Configuration Management, which can be used to record relationships between users and systems they can access.

7.4.5.4 Basic concepts of Access Management

Access Management should be utilized for providing/modifying and removing access rights to agreed services documented within the Service Catalog. The following definitions describe the major concepts involved with the process:

- **Access:** Refers to the level and extent of a service's functionality or data that a user is entitled to use.

- **Identity:** Refers to the information about them that distinguishes them as an individual and which verifies their status within the organization. By definition, the identity of the user is unique to that user.

- **Rights:** (Also called privileges) refer to the actual settings whereby a user is provided access to a service or group of services. Typical rights, or levels of access, include read, write, execute, change, delete.

- **Services or service groups**: Instead of providing access to each service for each user separately, it is more efficient to be able to grant each user access to a whole set of services that they are entitled to use at the same time.

- **Directory of services**: Refers to a specific type of tool that is used to manage access and rights.

7.5 Service Operation Summary

From a customer viewpoint, Service Operation is where actual value is seen. This is because it is the execution of strategies, designs and plans and improvements from the Service Lifecycle phases.

Key benefits delivered as a result of Service Operation are:
- Effectiveness and efficiency in IT Service delivery and support
- Increased return on investment
- More productive and positive users of IT services.

Other benefits can be defined as:

1. **Long term:** Over a period of time the Service Operation processes, functions performance and output are evaluated. These reports will be analyzed and decisions made about whether the improvement is needed, and how best to implement it through Service Design and Transition e.g. deployment of new tools, changes to process designs, reconfiguration of the infrastructure.

2. **Short term:** Improvement of working practices within the Service Operations processes, functions and technology itself. Generally they involve smaller improvements that do not mean changes to the fundamental nature of a process or technology e.g. tuning, training, personnel redeployment etc.

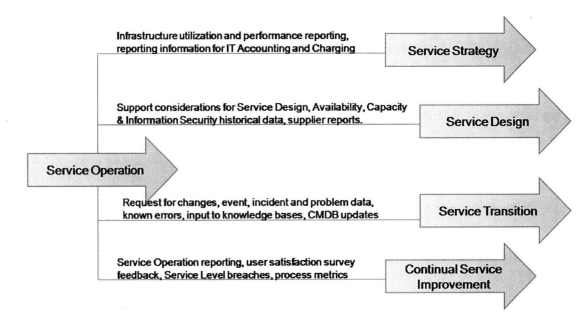

Figure 7.U – Some outputs to other lifecycle phases.

7.6 Service Operation Scenario

Functions

Service Desk

- Service desk has been trained in HYPE and can support users
- Has access to known errors and workarounds to resolve incidents.

Technical Management

- Designed, built, tested and rolled HYPE out into live environment
- Supports HYPE service.

Application Management

- Made modifications to HYPE application to ensure effectively interfaced with XY app
- Provided training on HYPE to users and Service Desk.

IT Operations Management

- Creates backups of logs, monitors component events.

Processes

Event Management

- Sends alerts to IT Ops when HYPE logs backups pass/fail
- Monitors thresholds for triggers on bandwidth (set up in Availability Management).

Request Fulfillment Management

- Users use this process to request copy of logs.

Access Management

- Password reset of HYPE account – provide authorized users access.

Incident Management and Problem Management are not discussed in this example.

7.7 Service Operation Review Questions

Question 1

What is the best definition of an Incident Model?

a) Predicting the impact of incidents on the network

b) A type of Incident that is used as a best practice model

c) A set of pre-defined steps to be followed when dealing with a known type of Incident

d) An Incident that requires a separate system

Question 2

What is the difference between a Known Error and a Problem?

a) The underlying cause of a Known Error is known. The underlying cause of a Problem is not known

b) A Known Error involves an error in the IT infrastructure. A Problem does not involve such an error.

c) A Known Error always originates from an Incident. This is not always the case with a Problem.

d) With a Problem, the relevant Configuration Items have been identified. This is not the case with a Known Error.

Question 3

Information is regularly exchanged between Problem Management and Change Management. What information is this?

a) Known Errors from Problem Management, on the basis of which Change Management can generate Requests for Change (RFCs)

b) RFCs resulting from Known Errors

c) RFCs from the users that Problem Management passes on to Change Management

d) RFCs from the Service Desk that Problem Management passes on to Change Management

Question 4

Incident Management has a value to the business by?

a) Helping to control cost of fixing technology

b) Enabling customers to resolve Problems

c) Helping to maximize business impact

d) Helping to reduce the business impact

Question 5

Which of the following is NOT an example of a Service Request?

a) A user calls the Service Desk to order a new mouse

b) A user calls the Service Desk because they would like to change the functionality of an application

c) A user calls the service desk to reset their password

d) A user logs onto an internal web site to download a licensed copy of software from a list of approved options

Question 6

The BEST definition of an event is?

a) A situation where a capacity threshold has been exceeded and an agreed Service Level has already been impacted

b) An occurrence that is significant for the management of the IT Infrastructure or delivery of services

c) A problem that requires immediate attention

d) A social gathering of IT staff to celebrate the release of a service

Question 7

Technical Management is NOT responsible for?

a) Maintenance of the local network

b) Identifying technical skills required to manage and support the IT Infrastructure

c) Defining the Service agreements for the technical infrastructure

d) Response to the disruption to the technical infrastructure

Question 8

Which of the following is NOT an objective of Service Operation?

a) Through testing, to ensure that services are designed to meet business needs

b) To deliver and support IT Services

c) To manage the technology used to deliver services

d) To monitor the performance of technology and processes

Question 9

Which of the following BEST describes the purpose of Event Management?

a) The ability to detect events, analyze them and determine the appropriate control action

b) The ability to coordinate changes in events

c) The ability to monitor and control projected service outages

d) The ability to report on success of all batch processing jobs

Question 10

Which process or function is responsible for management of the Data Center facility?

a) IT Operations Control

b) Supplier Management

c) Facilities Management

d) Technical Function

8 Continual Service Improvement

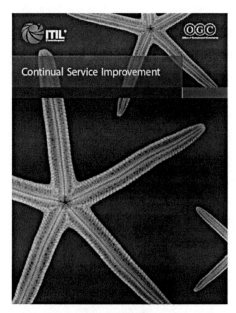

Figure 8.A – Continual Service Improvement

Processes:

- Service Measurement and Reporting

The main areas of focus for Continual Service Improvement to usually address are:

- The overall health of ITSM as a discipline
- Continual alignment of the portfolio of IT services with the current and future business needs
- Maturity of the enabling IT processes for each service in a continual service lifecycle model.

8.1 Objectives

To ensure continual improvements to IT Service Management Processes and IT Services (essentially anything within the scope of IT Service Management).

Continual Service Improvement is the phase that binds all the other elements of the Service Lifecycle together and ensures that both the services and the capabilities for providing them continually improves and matures.

8.2 Major Concepts

8.2.1 The Continual Service Improvement Model

The CSI Model provides the basis by which improvements to IT Service Management processes can be made. They are questions to ask in order to ensure all the required elements are identified to achieve the improvements desired.

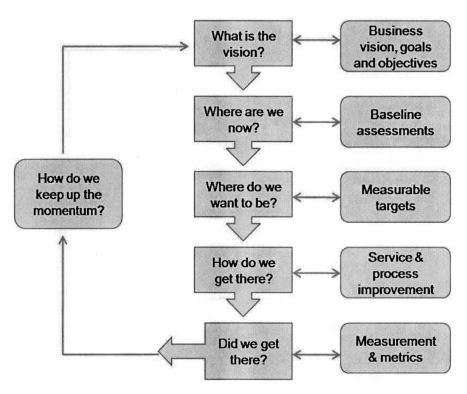

Figure 8.B: Continual Service Improvement Model

© Crown Copyright 2007 Reproduced under license from OGC

The Continual Service Improvement Model summarizes the constant cycle for improvement. While there may be a focus on a particular lifecycle phase, the questions require close interactions with all the other ITIL® processes in order to achieve Continual Service Improvement.

Example improvement initiative for Service Operation:

- **What is the Vision?** Defining what wants to be achieved by improving Service Operation. Is the focus on Service Quality, compliance, security, costs or customer satisfaction? What is the broad approach that we should take?

- **Where are we now?** Baselines taken by performing maturity assessments and by identifying what practices are currently being used (including informal and ad-hoc processes). What information can be provided by the Service Portfolio regarding strengths, weaknesses, risks and priorities of the Service Provider?

- **Where do we want to be?** Defining key goals and objectives that wish to be achieved by the formalization of Service Operation processes, including both short-term and long-term targets.

- **How do we get there?** Perform a gap analysis between the current practices and defined targets to begin developing plans to overcome these gaps. Typically the process owners and Service Operation manager will oversee the design/improvement of the processes, making sure they are fit for purpose and interface as needed with other Service Management processes.

- **Did we get there?** At agreed time schedules, checks should be made as to how the improvement initiatives have progressed. Which objectives have been achieved? Which haven't? What went well and what went wrong?

- **How do we keep the momentum going?** Now that the targets and objectives have been met, what is the next course of improvements that can be made? This should feed back into re-examining the vision and following the CSI model steps again.

Since Continual Service Improvement involves ongoing change, it is important to develop an effective communication strategy to support CSI activities and ensure people remain appropriately informed. This communication must include aspects of:

- What the service implications are
- What the impact on personnel will be
- Approach/process used to reach the objective.

If this communication does not exist, staff will fill the gaps with their own perceptions. Proper reporting should assist in addressing any misconceptions about improvements.

To aid understanding the differences in perception between the service provider and the customer, a Service Gap model can be used. This identifies the most obvious potential gaps in the service lifecycle from both a business and IT perspective.

SLM will produce Service Improvement Plans (SIPs) to meet the identified gaps.

8.2.2 Relationships within the Service Lifecycle:

- **What is the Vision?** Service Strategy, Service Portfolio
- **Where are we now?** Baselines taken using Service Portfolios, Service Level Management, and Financial Management for IT etc.
- **Where do we want to be?** Service Portfolio, Service Measurement and Reporting
- **How do we get there?** CSI and all ITIL® processes
- **Did we get there?** Service Measurement and Reporting
- **How do we keep the momentum going?** Continual Service Improvement.

8.2.3 The Deming Cycle

In the 1950s, W. Edwards Deming proposed that business processes should be analyzed and measured to identify sources of variations that cause products to deviate from customer requirements. He recommended that business processes be placed in a continuous feedback loop so that managers and supporting staff can identify and change the parts of the process that need improvements. As a theorist, Deming created a simplified model to illustrate this continuous process, commonly known as the PDCA cycle for Plan, Do, Check, Act:

- Plan: Design or revise business process components to improve results
- Do: Implement the plan and measure its performance

- Check: Assess the measurements and report the results to decision makers
- Act: Decide on changes needed to improve the process.

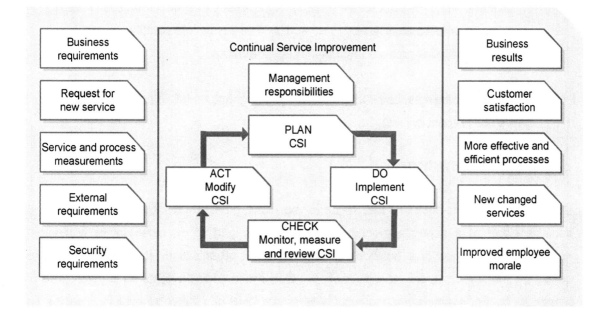

Figure 8.C: The Deming Cycle of Continual Improvement.
© Crown Copyright 2007 Reproduced under license from OGC

Too often organizations are looking for a big-bang approach to improvements. It is important to understand that a succession or series of small, planned increments of improvements will not stress the infrastructure as much and will eventually amount to a large amount of improvement over time.

So in relation to Continual Service Improvement, the PDCA model can be applied with the following steps.

1. Plan – scope, establishing goals, objectives and requirements, interfaces, process activities, framework of roles and responsibilities, appropriate tools, methods and techniques for measuring, assessing, analyzing and reporting.

2. Do (implement) – funding and budgets, documenting and allocation roles and responsibilities, documentation and maintaining CSI policies, plans and procedures,

communication and training, ensuring monitoring, analysis and trend evaluating and reporting tools is in place, integration with the other lifecycle phases.

3.   Check (monitor, measure, review) – reporting against plans, documentation review, conducting process assessments and audits. The key here is identifying and recommending CSI process improvement opportunities.

4.   Act – implementing actual CSI enhancements (e.g. updating CSI policies, procedures, roles and responsibilities).

8.2.4 IT Governance

Governance relates to decisions that define expectations, grant power, or verify performance. It consists either of a separate process or of a specific part of management or leadership processes. In the case of a business or of a non-profit organization, governance relates to consistent management, cohesive policies, processes and decision-rights for a given area of responsibility. For example, managing at a corporate level might involve evolving policies on privacy, on internal investment, and on the use of data.

There are 3 main areas of governance:

- **Enterprise governance** – Describes a framework that covers both corporate governance and the business management aspects of the organization. This achieves good corporate governance that is linked strategically with performance metrics, and enables companies to focus all their energy on the key drivers that move their business forward.

- **Corporate governance** – Concerned with promoting corporate fairness, transparency and accountability. One example is the SOX act (2002) in the United States; created in the aftermath of fraudulent behavior by corporate giants and states accountability provisions such as criminal charges and incarceration for non-compliance.

- **IT governance** – Responsibility of the board of directors and executive management. An integral part of enterprise governance and consists of the leadership, organizational structures and processes that ensure the organization's IT sustains and extends the organization's strategies and objectives.

8.3 Continual Service Improvement Processes

8.3.1 Service Measurement and Reporting

8.3.1.1 Goal and objectives

To coordinate the design of metrics, data collection and reporting activities from the other processes and functions.

There are four main reasons to monitor and measure:

- **Validate**:   Are we supporting the strategy and vision?
- **Direct**:   Based on factual data, people can be guided to change behavior
- **Justify**:   Do we have the right targets and metrics?
- **Intervene**:   Take corrective actions such as identifying improvement opportunities.

Measurement of all the process metrics takes place throughout all the Lifecycle phases. CSI uses the results of these measurements to identify and establish improvements via reports.

8.3.1.2 Types of Metrics

There are 3 types of metrics that an organization will need to collect to support CSI activities as well as other process activities:

- **Technology Metrics:** Often associated with component and application-based metrics such as performance, availability etc. The various design architects and technical specialists are responsible for defining the technology metrics.

- **Process Metrics:** Captured in the form of Key Performance Indicators (KPIs) and activity metrics for the service management processes which determine the overall health of a process. Four key questions KPIs can help answer are centered on quality, performance, value and compliance. CSI uses these metrics to identify improvement opportunities for each process. The various Process Owners are responsible for defining the metrics for the process they are responsible for coordinating and managing.

- **Service Metrics:** The results of the end-to-end service. Component metrics are used to calculate the service metrics. The Service Level Manager(s) and Service Owners are responsible for defining appropriate service metrics.

8.3.1.3 Baselines

A benchmark captured and used as a reference point for later comparison.

It is important that baselines as documents are recognized and accepted throughout the organization. Baseline must be established at each level: strategic goals, and objectives, tactical process maturity and operational metrics and KPIs.

Examples
1. A Service Level Achievement Baseline can be used as a starting point to measure the effect of a Service Improvement Plan.
2. A performance Baseline can be used to measure changes in performance over the lifetime of an IT service.
3. A Configuration Management baseline can be used to enable the IT infrastructure to be restored to a known configuration if a change or release fails.

8.3.1.4 Tension Metrics

All service providers are faced with the challenge with a balancing act of three main elements:
- Resources – people, IT infrastructure, consumables and money
- Features - the product or service and its quality
- Time schedule – the timeframes within which various stages and the final delivery of a service or product are required to be achieved.

The delivered product or service therefore represents a balanced trade-off between these three elements. Tension metrics can help create that balance by preventing teams from focusing on just one element. If an initiative is being driven primarily towards satisfying a business driver of on-time delivery to the exclusion of other factors, the manager will achieve this aim by flexing the resources and service features in order to meet the delivery schedule. This unbalanced focus will wither lead to budget increase or lower product quality. Tension metrics help create a balance between shared goals and delivering a product or service according to the business requirements within time and budget.

8.4 Continual Service Improvement Summary

There is great value to the business when service improvement takes a holistic approach throughout the entire lifecycle. Continual Service Improvement enables this holistic approach to be taken.

Some key benefits of the Continual Service Improvement phase:

- Increased growth
- Competitive Advantage
- Increased Return On Investment
- Increased Value On Investment.

ROI: Return on investment – Difference between the benefit (saving) achieved and the amount expended to achieve that benefit, expressed as percentage. Logically we would like to spend a little to save a lot.

VOI: Value on investment – Extra value created by establishment of benefits that include non-monetary or long term outcomes. ROI is a subcomponent of VOI.

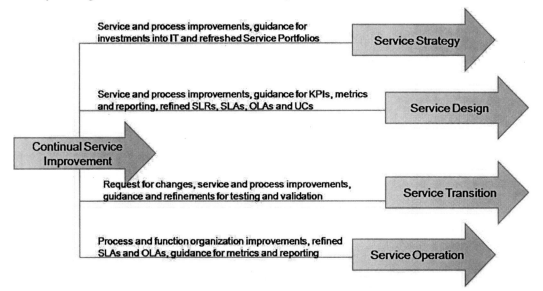

Figure 8.D – Some outputs to other lifecycle phases.

8.5 *Continual Service Improvement Scenario*

Service Measurement and Reporting

To do this effectively, it was necessary to take metrics and data and analyze this against targets.

The CSI improvement model was used as a roadmap for this SIP (Service Improvement Scenario). As the business needs changed, so had the perceived value of HYPE. HYPE had become an integral part of the business communication plan. As a result, new business plans/goals were established and new targets set, with an action plan for improvement.
This will identify:

- Technology improvements
- Process improvements
- Document improvements
- Training etc.

As plans were formalized and accepted by the business, Request for Changes to technology, process and documentation were submitted to Change Management.

And so it continues!

8.6 Continual Service Improvement Review Questions

Question 1

Why should monitoring and measuring be used when trying to improve services?

   a) To validate, justify, monitor and improve

   b) To validate, direct, justify and intervene

   c) To validate, check, act and improve

   d) To validate, analyze, direct and improve

Question 2

Which is the first activity of the Continual Service Improvement (CSI) model?

   a) Assess the customer's requirements

   b) Understand the vision of the business

   c) Identify what can be measured

   d) Develop a plan for improvement

Question 3

The four stages of the Deming Cycle are?

   a) Plan, Assess, Check, Report

   b) Plan, Do, Check, Act

   c) Plan, Check, Revise, Improve

   d) Plan, Do, Act, Assess

Question 4

Which of the following is NOT a step in the Continual Service Improvement (CSI) model?

   a) What is the vision?

   b) Did we get there?

   c) Who will help us get there?

   d) Where are we now?

Question 5

Which of the following provides the correct set of governance levels managed by an organization?

    a) Technology, Service, Business

    b) Financial, Legal, Security

    c) Process, Service, Technology

    d) IT, Corporate, Enterprise

9 ITIL® Foundation Exam Tips

Exam Details:

- 40 questions
- The correct answer is only one of the four
- 60 minutes duration
- 26 out of 40 is a pass (65%)
- Closed book
- No notes

Practical Suggestions:

- Read the question CAREFULLY

- At this level of exam the obvious answer is often the correct answer *(if you have read the question carefully!!)*

- Beware of being misled by the preliminary text for the question

- If you think there should be another choice that would be the right answer, then you have to choose the "most right"

- Use strategies such as *"What comes first?"* or *"What doesn't belong?"* to help with the more difficult questions

- Where there are questions that involve multiple statements (i.e. 1, 2, 3, 4), then try to eliminate combinations that are immediately incorrect (based on something you can remember) so that the question is broken into smaller, and more manageable pieces.

Make sure that you prepare adequately in the lead up to your exam by reviewing your notes, reading any available material and attempting the sample exams.

We hope this book has been of value, and wish you luck in your exam and future IT Service Management career!

10 Answers for review questions

The following section provides example reasoning for each answer. This is only a guide however, and does not cover every possible reason why an answer is correct or incorrect.

10.1 Service Strategy

ANSWERS

1c, 2a, 3b, 4c, 5b, 6a, 7d, 8b, 9b, 10d

Question 1

Which ITIL® process is responsible for developing a charging system?
   a) Availability Management
   b) Capacity Management
   c) **Financial Management for IT Services - *This is an element of IT accounting and chargeback***
   d) Service Level Management – *While SLM does assist, SLM will only review the charges with customers, rather than developing the charging model itself.*

Question 2

What is the RACI model used for?
   a) **Documenting the roles and relationships of stakeholders in a process or activity – *this is the primary purpose of RACI, i.e. mapping processes to functions and roles.***
   b) Defining requirements for a new service or process – *not the purpose of RACI*
   c) Analyzing the business impact of an incident - *not the purpose of RACI*
   d) Creating a balanced scorecard showing the overall status of Service Management - *not the purpose of RACI*

Question 3

Which of the following identifies two Service Portfolio components within the Service Lifecycle?
   a) Catalogue Service Knowledge Management System and Requirements Portfolio
   b) **Service Catalogue and Service Pipeline – *correct, the three areas are Pipeline, Catalogue and Retired Services.***

c) Service Knowledge Management System and Service Catalogue

d) Service Pipeline and Configuration Management System

Question 4

Which of the following is NOT one of the ITIL® core publications?

a) Service Operation

b) Service Transition

c) Service Derivation

d) Service Strategy

Question 5

A Service Level Package is best described as?

a) A description of customer requirements used to negotiate a Service Level Agreement – *These are Service Level Requirements*

b) A defined level of utility and warranty associated with a core service package – *Correct, a combination of utility and warranty that meets the customer's needs.*

c) A description of the value that the customer wants and for which they are willing to pay

d) A document showing the Service Levels achieved during an agreed reporting period – *These are Service Level Achievements*

Question 6

Setting policies and objectives is the primary concern of which of the following elements of the Service Lifecycle?

a) Service Strategy – Correct, *see objectives of Service Strategy*

b) Service Strategy and Continual Service Improvement

c) Service Strategy, Service Transition and Service Operation

d) Service Strategy, Service Design, Service Transition, Service Operation and Continual Service Improvement

Question 7

A service owner is responsible for which of the following?

a) Designing and documenting a Service – *normally the role of Service Architects*

b) Carrying out the Service Operations activities needed to support a Service – normally *Service Desk and other operational staff*

c) Producing a balanced scorecard showing the overall status of all Services – *Service owner isn't responsible for ALL services*

d) Recommending improvements – *Correct, the Service Owner is responsible for continually improving their service.*

Question 8

The utility of a service is best described as:

a) Fit for design

b) Fit for purpose

c) Fit for function

d) Fit for use – this is warranty (i.e. performance, availability etc.)

Question 9

The 4 P's of ITSM are people, partners, processes and …?:

a) Purpose

b) Products – *Correct, see introduction to IT Service Management.*

c) Perspectives

d) Practice

Question 10

The contents of a service package includes:

a) Base Service Package, Supporting Service Package, Service Level Package

b) Core Service Package, Supporting Process Package, Service Level Package

c) Core Service Package, Base Service Package, Service Support Package

d) Core Service Package, Supporting Services Package, Service Level Packages – *Correct, see Service Packages*

10.2 Service Design

ANSWERS

1b, 2a, 3d, 4d, 5b, 6b, 7a, 8b, 9c, 10d

Question 1

Which ITIL® process analyses threats and dependencies to IT Services as part of the decision regarding "countermeasures" to be implemented?

a) Availability Management – *concerned with operational disruptions and the measures for recovery (i.e. redundant components), rather than specific recovery environments and countermeasures.*

b) IT Service Continuity Management

c) Problem Management – *will investigate the cause of a disruption, but only contributes to recovery planning.*

d) Service Asset & Configuration Management – *only records and provides the information, does not analyze and evaluate anything itself.*

Question 2

What is the name of the activity within the Capacity Management process whose purpose is to predict the future capacity requirements of new and changed services?

a) Application Sizing

b) Demand Management – this is a separate process, analyzing how business demand will change over time.

c) Modeling – *this is a separate activity, estimating the performance of the infrastructure under certain conditions*

d) Tuning

Question 3

In which ITIL® process are negotiations held with customers about the availability and capacity levels to be provided?

a) Availability Management

b) Capacity Management

c) Financial Management for IT Services

d) **Service Level Management –** *SLM is always the process that negotiates with customers about any aspect of service quality.*

Question 4

Which of the following statements is false?

a) It is impossible to maintain user and customer satisfaction during a disruption to service.

b) When reporting the availability provided for a service, the percentage (%) availability that is calculated takes into account the agreed service hours. *See measuring Availability*

c) Availability of services could be improved by changes to the architecture, ITSM processes or IT staffing levels. *See incident lifecycle, for increasing uptime and reducing downtime.*

d) **Reports regarding availability should include more than just uptime, downtime and frequency of failure, and reflect the actual business impact of unavailability.** *Correct, this is called business oriented availability reporting.*

Question 5

Which of the following activities is Service Level Management responsible for?

a) Informing users of available services – *this is the role of the Service Desk*

b) **Identifying customer needs**

c) Overseeing service release schedule – This is the role of Release & Deployment process

d) Keeping accurate records of all configuration items – *Service Asset & Configuration Management*

Question 6

Which process reviews Operational Level Agreements (OLAs) on a regular basis?

a) Supplier Management – *reviews Underpinning Contracts*

b) **Service Level Management**

c) Service Portfolio Management

d) Contract Management – *not an ITIL process, this is included within Supplier Management.*

Question 7

What is another term for Uptime?

    a) **Mean Time Between Failures (MTBF)**

    b) Mean Time to Restore Service (MTRS) - *downtime*

    c) Mean Time Between System Incidents (MTBSI) – *frequency of failures*

    d) Relationship between MTBF and MTBSI

Question 8

Which of the following is an activity of IT Service Continuity Management?

    a) Advising end users of a system failure – *Service Desk's role during a crisis.*

    b) **Documenting the recovery procedure for a critical system** – *Correct, this is an activity of the ITSCM process*

    c) Reporting regarding availability – *This is an activity of Availability Management*

    d) Guaranteeing that the Configuration Items are constantly kept up-to-date.

Question 9

Information security must consider the following four perspectives:

    1. Organizational

    2. Physical

    3. Technical

    4. ?

    a) Process

    b) Security

    c) **Procedural** – *See scope of Information Security Management*

    d) Firewalls

Question 10

The 3 types of Service Level Agreements structures are:

    a) Customer based, Service based, Corporate based

    b) Corporate level, customer level, service level

    c) Service based, customer based, user based

    d) **Customer based, service based, multi-level**

10.3 Service Transition

ANSWERS

1a, 2b, 3d, 3b, 5b, 6c, 7a, 8b, 9a, 10b

Question 1

The key element of a standard change is: ?

a) **Documentation of a pre-approved procedure for implementing the change**

b) Low risk to the production environment – *this in itself doesn't guarantee a standard change.*

c) No requirement for service downtime – *the risk of unplanned disruption may still be high.*

d) It can be included in the next monthly or quarterly release. *This relates to the packaging of releases, not the classification of changes.*

Question 2

Release and deployment options include:

1. Big bang vs. Phased

2. Automated vs. Manual

3. ?

a) Push vs. Proposed

b) **Push vs. Pull**

c) Requested vs. Forced

d) Proposed vs. Forced

Question 3

The 4 spheres of knowledge management are:

a) Data, facts, knowledge, wisdom

b) Ideas, facts knowledge, wisdom

c) Data, information, facts, wisdom

d) **Data, information, knowledge, wisdom – *easier to remember as DIKW***

Question 4

Which activity in Service Asset & Configuration Management would help to ascertain whether the recorded Configuration Items conform to the physical environment?

    a) Control – *this is the actual modification of CIs themselves*

    b) Verification and audit

    c) Identification – *this collects all the information to be stored for a CI*

    d) Status accounting – *this doesn't itself doesn't include validation procedures.*

Question 5

After a Change has been implemented, an evaluation is performed. What is this evaluation called?

    a) Forward Schedule of Changes (FSC)

    b) Post Implementation Review (PIR)

    c) Service Improvement Program (SIP)

    d) Service Level Requirement (SLR)

Question 6

Which of the following is not change type?

    a) Standard change

    b) Normal change

    c) Quick change

    d) Emergency change

Question 7

Which process is responsible for maintaining software items in the Definitive Media Library (DML)?

    a) Release and Deployment Management – *as R&D will be responsible for storing and deploying all software items in the DML*

    b) Service Asset and Configuration Management – *only responsible for maintaining the records associated with the DML*

    c) Service validation and testing

    d) Change Management

Question 8

Which process or function is responsible for communicating the Change Schedule to the users?

a) Change Management – *responsible for maintaining the Change Schedule, but provides this to the Service Desk for communicating to users.*

b) Service Desk – *should be the single point of contact for ALL user communication*

c) Release and Deployment Management

d) Service Level Management

Question 9

Which of the following best describes a baseline?

a) Used as a reference point for later comparison

b) The starting point of any project – *only one example of a baseline*

c) The end point of any project – *only one example of a baseline*

d) A rollback procedure

Question 10

The main objective of Change Management is to?

a) Ensure that any changes are approved and recorded – *not all changes are approved.*

b) Ensure that standardized methods and procedures are used for controlled handling of all changes

c) Ensure that any change requests are managed through the CAB – *this is not true for standard changes*

d) Ensure that the CAB takes responsibility for all change implementation – *CAB only coordinates implementation, the work is performed within the Release & Deployment process.*

10.4 Service Operation

ANSWERS

1c, 2a, 3b, 4d, 5b, 6b, 7c, 8a, 9a, 10c

Question 1

What is the best definition of an Incident Model?

a) Predicting the impact of incidents on the network

b) A type of Incident that is used as a best practice model

c) A set of pre-defined steps to be followed when dealing with a known type of Incident

d) An Incident that requires a separate system

Question 2

What is the difference between a Known Error and a Problem?

a) The underlying cause of a Known Error is known. The underlying cause of a Problem is not known

b) A Known Error involves an error in the IT infrastructure. A Problem does not involve such an error.

c) A Known Error always originates from an Incident. This is not always the case with a Problem.

d) With a Problem, the relevant Configuration Items have been identified. This is not the case with a Known Error. – *explanation is reversed*

Question 3

Information is regularly exchanged between Problem Management and Change Management. What information is this?

a) Known Errors from Problem Management, on the basis of which Change Management can generate Requests for Change (RFCs) – *Change Management accepts the RFC, doesn't create it itself.*

b) RFCs resulting from Known Errors

c) RFCs from the users that Problem Management passes on to Change Management

d) RFCs from the Service Desk that Problem Management passes on to Change Management

Question 4

Incident Management has a value to the business by?

    a) Helping to control cost of fixing technology

    b) Enabling customers to resolve Problems – *This is problem management*

    c) Helping to maximize business impact

    d) Helping to reduce the business impact

Question 5

Which of the following is NOT an example of a Service Request?

    a) A user calls the Service Desk to order a new mouse

    b) A user calls the Service Desk because they would like to change the functionality of an application – *this would be a Normal Change, due to the potential risk and implications of the change.*

    c) A user calls the service desk to reset their password

    d) A user logs onto an internal web site to download a licensed copy of software from a list of approved options – this is an example of a service request workflow that has been automated.

Question 6

The BEST definition of an event is?

    a) A situation where a capacity threshold has been exceeded and an agreed Service Level has already been impacted – *only one type of event (exception)*

    b) An occurrence that is significant for the management of the IT Infrastructure or delivery of services

    c) A problem that requires immediate attention

    d) A social gathering of IT staff to celebrate the release of a service

Question 7

Technical Management is NOT responsible for?

    a) Maintenance of the local network

    b) Identifying technical skills required to manage and support the IT Infrastructure

    c) **Defining the Service agreements for the technical infrastructure –** *this is the role of Service Level Management*

    d) *Response to the disruption to the technical infrastructure*

Question 8

Which of the following is NOT an objective of Service Operation?

    a) **Through testing, to ensure that services are designed to meet business needs –** *this is an objective of Service Transition*

    b) To deliver and support IT Services

    c) To manage the technology used to deliver services

    d) To monitor the performance of technology and processes

Question 9

Which of the following BEST describes the purpose of Event Management?

    a) **The ability to detect events, analyze them and determine the appropriate control action**

    b) The ability to coordinate changes in events

    c) The ability to monitor and control projected service outages – *this is only one role of Event Management*

    d) The ability to report on success of all batch processing jobs – *this is only one role of Event Management*

Question 10

Which process or function is responsible for management of the Data centre facility?

    a) IT Operations Control

    b) Supplier Management

    c) **Facilities Management**

    d) Technical Function

10.5 Continual Service Improvement

ANSWERS

1b, 2b, 3b, 4c, 5a

Question 1

Why should monitoring and measuring be used when trying to improve services?

a) To validate, justify, monitor and improve

b) To validate, direct, justify and intervene – *See Service Measurement & Reporting*

c) To validate, check, act and improve

d) To validate, analyze, direct and improve

Question 2

Which is the first activity of the Continual Service Improvement (CSI) model?

a) Assess the customer's requirements

b) Understand the vision of the business

c) Identify what can be measured

d) Develop a plan for improvement

Question 3

The four stages of the Deming Cycle are?

a) Plan, Assess, Check, Report

b) Plan, Do, Check, Act

c) Plan, Check, Revise, Improve

d) Plan, Do, Act, Assess

Question 4

Which of the following is NOT a step in the Continual Service Improvement (CSI) model?

a) What is the vision?

b) Did we get there?

c) Who will help us get there?

d) Where are we now?

Question 5

Which of the following provides the correct set of governance levels managed by an organization?

    a) Technology, Service, Business

    b) Financial, Legal, Security

    c) Process, Service, Technology

    d) IT, Corporate, Enterprise

11 Glossary

Term	Definition
Accounting	In the context of ITSM, this is a synonym for IT Accounting.
Agreement	A Document that describes a formal understanding between two or more parties. An Agreement is not legally binding, unless it forms part of a Contract.
Application Management	The Process responsible for managing Applications throughout their Lifecycle.
Asset Management	**(Financial Management)** Asset Management is the Business Process responsible for tracking and reporting the value and ownership of financial Assets throughout their Lifecycle.
Availability	**(Availability Management) (Security Management)** Ability of a Configuration Item or IT Service to perform its agreed Function when required. Availability is determined by Reliability, Maintainability, Serviceability, Performance, and Security. Availability is usually calculated as a percentage. This calculation is often based on Agreed Service Time and Downtime. It is Best Practice to calculate Availability using measurements of the Business output of the IT Service. See Security Principle.
Availability Management	**(Availability Management)** The Process responsible for defining, analyzing, Planning, measuring and improving all aspects of the Availability of IT services. Availability Management is responsible for ensuring that all IT Infrastructure, Processes, Tools, Roles etc are appropriate for the agreed Service Level Targets for Availability.

Term	Definition
Baseline	The recorded state of something at a specific point in time. A Baseline can be created for a Configuration, a Process, or any other set of data. For example, a baseline can be used in: • Continuous Service Improvement, to establish a starting point for planning improvements. • Capacity Management, to document performance characteristics during normal operations. • Configuration Management, to enable the IT Infrastructure to be restored to a known configuration if a Change fails. Also used to specify a standard Configuration for data capture, release or Audit purposes.
Budgeting	**(Financial Management)** The Activity of predicting and controlling the spending of money. Consists of a periodic negotiation cycle to set future Budgets (usually annual) and the day-to-day monitoring and adjusting of current Budgets.
Build	**(Release Management)** The Activity of assembling a number of Configuration Items to create part of an IT Service. The term Build is also used to refer to a Release that is authorized for distribution. For example Server Build or laptop Build.
Business Continuity Plan (BCP)	**(IT Service Continuity Management)** A Plan defining the steps required to Restore Business Processes following a disruption. The Plan will also identify the triggers for Invocation, people to be involved, communications etc. IT Service Continuity Plans form a significant part of Business Continuity Plans.
Business Impact Analysis (BIA)	**(IT Service Continuity Management)** BIA is the Activity in Business Continuity Management that identifies Vital Business Functions and their dependencies. These dependencies may include Suppliers, people, other Business Processes, IT Services etc. BIA defines the recovery requirements for IT Services. These requirements include Recovery Time Objectives, Recovery Point Objectives and minimum Service Level Targets for each IT Service.

Term	Definition
Business Relationship Management (BRM)	**(Business Relationship Management)** The Process responsible for maintaining a Relationship with the Business. This Process usually includes: • Managing personal Relationships with Business managers • Portfolio Management • Ensuring that the IT Service Provider is satisfying the Business needs of the Customers This Process has strong links with Service Level Management.
Capacity	**(Capacity Management)** The maximum Throughput that a Configuration Item or IT Service can deliver whilst meeting agreed Service Level Targets. For some types of CI, Capacity may be the size or volume, for example a disk drive.
Capacity Management	**(Capacity Management)** The Process responsible for ensuring that the Capacity of IT Services and the IT Infrastructure is able to deliver agreed Service Level Targets in a Cost Effective and timely manner. Capacity Management considers all Resources required to deliver the IT Service, and plans for short, medium and long term Business Requirements.
Change	**(Change Management)** The addition, modification or removal of anything that could have an effect on IT Services. The Scope should include all Configuration Items, Processes, Documentation etc.
Change Advisory Board (CAB)	**(Change Management)** A group of people that assists the Change Manager in the assessment, prioritization and scheduling of Changes. This board is usually made up of representatives from all areas within the IT Service Provider, representatives from the Business, and Third Parties such as Suppliers.
Change Advisory Board / Emergency Committee (CAB/EC)	**(Change Management)** A sub-set of the Change Advisory Board who make decisions about Emergency Changes. Membership of the CAB/EC may be decided at the time a meeting is called, and depends on the nature of the Emergency Change.
Change Management	**(Change Management)** The Process responsible for controlling the Lifecycle of all Changes. The primary objective of Change Management is to enable beneficial Changes to be made, with minimum disruption to IT Services.
Charging	**(Financial Management)** Requiring payment for IT Services. Charging for IT Services is optional, and many Organizations choose to treat their IT Service Provider as a Cost Centre.

Term	Definition
Configuration Item (CI)	**(Configuration Management)** Any Component that needs to be managed in order to deliver an IT Service. Information about each CI is recorded in a Configuration Record within the CMDB and is maintained throughout its Lifecycle by Configuration Management. CIs are under the control of Change Management. CIs typically include hardware, software, buildings, people, and formal documentation such as Process documentation and SLAs.
Configuration Management	**(Configuration Management)** The Process responsible for maintaining information about Configuration Items required to deliver an IT Service, including their Relationships. This information is managed throughout the Lifecycle of the CI. The primary objective of Configuration Management is to underpin the delivery of IT Services by providing accurate data to all IT Service Management Processes when and where it is needed.
Configuration Management Database (CMDB)	**(Configuration Management)** A Database used to manage Configuration Records throughout their Lifecycle. The CMDB records the Attributes of each CI, and Relationships with other CIs. A CMDB may also contain other information linked to CIs, for example Incident, Problem or Change Records. The CMDB is maintained by Configuration Management and is used by all IT Service Management Processes.
Cost	**(Financial Management)** The amount of money spent on a specific Activity, IT Service, or Business Unit. Costs consist of real cost (money), notional cost such as people's time, and Depreciation. Cost is also used as the name of a Charging Policy that recovers the exact cost of providing the service.
Critical Success Factor (CSF)	Something that must happen if a Process, Project, Plan, or IT Service is to succeed. KPIs are used to measure the achievement of each CSF. For example a CSF of "protect IT Services when making Changes" could be measured by KPIs such as "percentage reduction of unsuccessful Changes", "percentage reduction in Changes causing Incidents" etc.
Customer	Someone who buys goods or Services. The Customer of an IT Service Provider is the person or group who defines and agrees the Service Level Targets. The term Customers is also sometimes informally used to mean Users, for example "this is a Customer Focused Organization".

Term	Definition
Definitive Hardware Store (DHS)	**(Release Management)** One or more physical locations in which hardware Configuration Items are securely stored when not in use. All hardware in the DHS is under the control of Change and Release Management and is recorded in the CMDB. The DHS contains spare parts, maintained at suitable revision levels, and may also include hardware that is part of a future Release.
Definitive Software Library (DSL)	**(Release Management)** One or more locations in which the definitive and approved versions of all software Configuration Items are securely stored. The DSL may also contain associated CIs such as licenses and documentation. The DSL is a single logical storage area even if there are multiple locations. All software in the DSL is under the control of Change and Release Management and is recorded in the CMDB. Only software from the DSL is acceptable for use in a Release.
Demand Management	**(Capacity Management)** Optimizing the use of Capacity by moving Workload to less utilized times, Servers, or places. Demand Management often uses Differential Charging to encourage Customers to use IT Services at less busy times. Demand Management also makes use of other techniques such as limiting the number of concurrent Users.
Emergency Change	**(Change Management)** A Change that must be introduced as soon as possible. For example to resolve a Major Incident or implement a Security patch. The Change Management Process will normally have a specific Procedure for handling Emergency Changes.
Financial Management for IT Services	**(Financial Management)** The Process responsible for managing an IT Service Provider's Budgeting, Accounting and Charging requirements.
Help Desk	**(Service Desk)** A point of contact for Users to log Incidents. A Help Desk is usually more technically focused than a Service Desk and does not provide a Single Point of Contact for all interaction. The term Help Desk is often used as a synonym for Service Desk.
Incident	**(Incident Management)** An unplanned interruption to an IT Service or reduction in the Quality of an IT Service. Any event which could affect an IT Service in the future is also an Incident. For example Failure of one disk from a mirror set.
Incident Management	**(Incident Management)** The Process responsible for managing the Lifecycle of all Incidents. The primary Objective of Incident Management is to return the IT Service to Customers as quickly as possible.

Term	Definition
Information Technology (IT)	The use of technology for the storage, communication or processing of information. The technology typically includes computers, telecommunications, Applications and other software. The information may include Business data, voice, images, video, etc. Information Technology is often used to support Business Processes through IT Services.
IT Infrastructure Library (ITIL)	A set of Best Practice guidance for IT Service Management. ITIL is owned by the OGC and is developed in conjunction with the itSMF. ITIL consists of a series of publications giving guidance on the provision of Quality IT Services, and on the Processes and facilities needed to support them. See http://www.ogc.gov.uk/index.asp?id=2261 for more information.
Key Performance Indicator (KPI)	A Metric that is used to help manage a Process, IT Service or Activity. Many Metrics may be measured, but only the most important of these are defined as KPIs and used to actively manage and report on the Process, IT Service or Activity. KPIs should be selected to ensure that Efficiency, Effectiveness, and Cost Effectiveness are all managed.
Knowledge Management	The Process responsible for gathering, analyzing, storing and sharing knowledge information within an Organization. The primary purpose of Knowledge Management is to improve Efficiency by reducing the need to rediscover knowledge.
Known Error (KE)	**(Problem Management)** A Problem that has a documented Root Cause and a Workaround. Known Errors are created by Problem Control and are managed throughout their Lifecycle by Error Control. Known Errors may also be identified by Development or Suppliers.
Known Error Database	**(Service Desk) (Incident Management) (Problem Management)** A Database containing all Known Error Records. This Database is created by Problem Management and used by Incident and Problem Management.

Term	Definition
Lifecycle	The various stages in the life of a Configuration Item, Incident, Problem, Change etc. The Lifecycle defines the Categories for Status and the Status transitions that are permitted. For example: • The Lifecycle of an Application includes Design, Build, Test, Deploy, Operate etc. • The lifecycle of an Incident includes Detect, Respond, Diagnose, Repair, Recover, Restore. • The lifecycle of a Server may include: Ordered, Received, In Test, Live, Disposed etc.
Major Incident	**(Incident Management)** The highest Category of Impact for an Incident. A Major Incident results in significant disruption to the Business.
Operational Level Agreement (OLA)	**(Service Level Management)** An Agreement between an IT Service Provider and another part of the same Business that provides Services to them. For example there could be an OLA with a facilities department to provide air conditioning, or with the procurement department to obtain hardware in agreed times. An OLA may also be between two parts of the same IT Service Provider, for example between the Service Desk and a Support Group.
Policy	Formally documented management expectations and intentions. Policies are used to direct decisions, and to ensure consistent and appropriate development and implementation of Processes, Standards, Roles, Activities, IT Infrastructure etc.
Proactive Problem Management	**(Problem Management)** Part of the Problem Management Process. The Objective of Proactive Problem Management is to identify Problems that might otherwise be missed. Proactive Problem Management analyses Incident Records, and uses data collected by other IT Service Management Processes to identify trends or significant problems.
Problem	The root cause of one or more incidents.
Problem Management	**(Problem Management)** The Process responsible for managing the Lifecycle of all Problems. The primary objectives of Problem Management are to prevent Incidents from happening, and to minimize the Impact of Incidents that cannot be prevented. Problem Management includes Problem Control, Error Control and Proactive Problem Management.

©The Art of Service

Term	Definition
Release	**(Release Management)** A collection of hardware, software, documentation, Processes or other Components required to implement one or more approved Changes to IT Services. The contents of each Release are managed, tested, and deployed as a single entity.
Release Management	**(Release Management)** The Process responsible for Planning, scheduling and controlling the movement of Releases to Test and Live Environments. The primary objective of Release Management is to ensure that the integrity of the Live Environment is protected and that the correct Components are released. Release Management works closely with Configuration Management and Change Management.
Request for Change (RFC)	**(Change Management)** A formal proposal for a Change to be made. An RFC includes details of the proposed Change, and may be recorded on paper or electronically. The term RFC is often misused to mean a Change Record, or the Change itself.
Return on Investment (ROI)	**(Financial Management)** A measurement of the expected benefit of an investment. Calculated by dividing the average increase in financial benefit (taken over an agreed number of years) by the investment.
Risk	The possibility of suffering harm or loss. In quantitative Risk Management this is calculated as how likely it is that a specific Threat will exploit a particular Vulnerability.
Risk Assessment	The initial steps of Risk Management. Analyzing the value of Assets to the business, identifying Threats to those Assets, and evaluating how Vulnerable each Asset is to those Threats.
Risk Management	The Process responsible for identifying, assessing and managing Risks. Risk Management can be quantitative (based on numerical data) or qualitative.
Service Catalog	A Document listing all IT Services, with summary information about their SLAs and Customers. The Service Catalogue is created and maintained by the IT Service Provider and is used by all IT Service Management Processes.

Term	Definition
Service Desk	**(Service Desk)** The Single Point of Contact between the Service Provider and the Users. A typical Service Desk manages Incidents and Service Requests, and also handles communication with the Users.
Service Level Agreement (SLA)	**(Service Level Management)** An Agreement between an IT Service Provider and a Customer. The SLA describes the IT Service, documents Service Level Targets, and specifies the responsibilities of the IT Service Provider and the Customer. A single SLA may cover multiple IT Services or multiple customers.
Service Level Management (SLM)	**(Service Level Management)** The Process responsible for negotiating Service Level Agreements, and ensuring that these are met. SLM is responsible for ensuring that all IT Service Management Processes, Operational Level Agreements, and Underpinning Contracts, are appropriate for the agreed Service Level Targets. SLM monitors and reports on Service Levels, and holds regular Customer reviews.
Single Point of Contact (SPOC)	Providing a single consistent way to communicate with an Organization or Business Unit. For example, a Single Point of Contact for an IT Service Provider is usually called a Service Desk.
Single Point of Failure (SPOF)	Any Configuration Item that can cause an Incident when it fails, and for which a Countermeasure has not been implemented. A SPOF may be a person, or a step in a Process or Activity, as well as a Component of the IT Infrastructure.
Standard Change	A pre-approved Change that is low Risk, relatively common and follows a Procedure or Work Instruction. For example password reset or provision of standard equipment to a new employee. RFCs are not required to implement a Standard Change, and they are logged and tracked using a different mechanism, such as a Service Request.
Underpinning Contract (UC)	A Contract with an external Third Party that supports delivery of an IT Service by the IT Service Provider to a Customer. The Third Party provides goods or Services that are required by the IT Service Provider to meet agreed Service Level Targets in the SLA with their Customer.

Term	Definition
Urgency	A measure of how long it will be until an Incident, Problem or Change has a significant Impact on the Business. For example a high Impact Incident may have low Urgency, if the Impact will not affect the Business until the end of the Financial Year. Impact and Urgency are used to assign Priority.
User	A person who uses the IT Service on a day-to-day basis. Users are distinct from Customers, as some Customers do not use the IT Service directly.
Vital Business Function (VBF)	A Function of a Business Process which is critical to the success of the Business. Vital Business Functions are an important consideration of Business Continuity Management, IT Service Continuity Management and Availability Management.
Workaround	**(Incident Management) (Problem Management)** Reducing or eliminating the Impact of an Incident or Problem for which a full Resolution is not yet available. For example by restarting a failed Configuration Item. Workarounds for Problems are documented in Known Error Records. Workarounds for Incidents that do not have associated Problem Records are documented in the Incident Record.

12 Certification

12.1 ITIL® Certification Pathways

There are many pathway options that are available once you have acquired your ITIL® Foundation Certification.   Below illustrates the possible pathways that are available to you. Currently it is intended that the highest certification is the ITIL® V3 Expert, considered to be equal to that of Diploma Status.

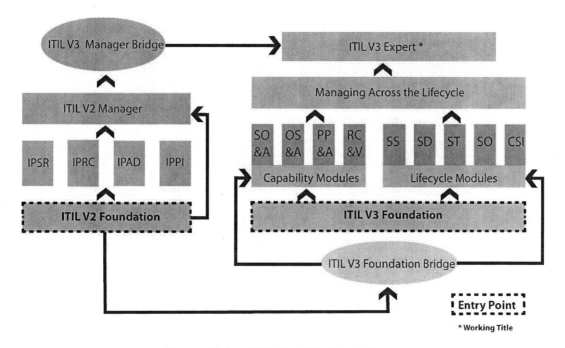

Figure 12.A – ITIL® Certification Pathway

For more information on certification and available programs please visit our website http://theartofservice.com.

12.2 ISO/IEC 20000 Pathways

ISO/IEC 20000 Standard is becoming a basic requirement for IT Service providers and is fast becoming the most recognized symbol of quality regarding IT Service Management processes. Once you have acquired your ITIL® Foundation Certification, you are eligible to pursue the ISO/IEC 20000 certification pathways. ISO/IEC 20000 programs aim to assist IT professionals master and understand the standard itself and issues relating to earning actual standards compliance.

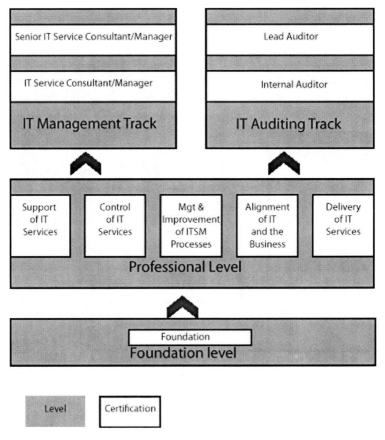

Figure 12.B – ISO/IEC 20000 Certification Pathway

For more information on certification and available programs please visit our website http://theartofservice.com.

13 Index

A

Access Management   8, 199, 202-3, 207
accounting   46, 76, 225, 239
agreements   65-7, 69, 75, 80, 88, 101, 103, 107, 239, 245, 247
alignment   6, 13, 15, 72
applications   1, 19, 22-3, 51, 75, 83, 94, 125, 135, 150, 173-4, 198-9, 209, 235, 239, 244-5
architectures   62-3, 87, 118, 157, 173, 229
assessment   93, 136-7, 140, 241
assets   20, 45, 102, 132, 149, 202, 246
attributes   6, 11, 45, 56, 127, 130, 152, 242
audits   110, 129, 131, 153, 216, 232
availability   28-9, 36, 51, 56-7, 92-6, 98-9, 106, 117-18, 122, 161, 173, 180, 202, 217, 227-9, 239
Availability Management   7, 15, 59, 92-4, 97, 99-100, 115, 117, 179, 202-3, 207, 225, 228, 230, 239
awareness   99, 101, 104, 110

B

balance   41, 44, 47-8, 113, 123, 133, 136, 140, 156, 158-9, 179, 219
balanced scorecard   59-60, 225-6
baselines   88, 155, 213-14, 218, 233, 240
benefits   2-3, 12-13, 21, 34, 36, 45, 48, 55, 88, 121-3, 131, 133, 140, 151, 162-5, 220
book   1-3, 31, 57, 224
budgets   10, 48, 55, 80, 121, 215, 219, 240
business units   21, 49-50, 53, 82, 186, 242, 247

C

CAB (Change Advisory Board)   136, 139, 142, 152, 155, 233, 241
capabilities   10-11, 19-20, 33, 35, 40-2, 45, 48, 53, 63, 65, 75, 85, 92, 120, 125, 127
capacity   28-9, 36, 38, 40, 48-51, 53-4, 57, 85, 87-8, 90, 181, 197, 241, 243
Capacity Management   7, 15, 48, 59, 85-91, 117, 182, 197, 225, 228, 241, 243
catalog   3, 78
certification   9, 249-50
Certification Pathway   9, 249-50
Change Management   7, 104, 120, 133-6, 138-40, 143, 145, 150, 152, 154-5, 194, 199-201, 203, 208, 232-4, 241
changes, standard   136-7, 139, 153-4, 199, 201, 231-3, 247
CI (Configuration Item)   19, 78, 81-2, 94-7, 118-19, 123, 127-8, 130, 132, 135, 145, 152-3, 229-30, 232, 239-43, 247-8
CMDB (Configuration Management Database)   128-31, 134, 145, 242-3
CMMI (Capability Maturity Model Integrated)   18
CMS (Configuration Management System)   78, 81-2, 126, 128-9, 144-5
communication   25, 34-5, 46, 80, 82, 105, 110, 161, 190, 213-14, 216, 233, 240, 244, 247
compliance   104, 107, 128, 131, 201, 213, 218

Component Capacity Management   88

concepts   6, 19, 22, 28, 30-1, 35, 74, 94, 96, 125

Configuration Management   7, 56, 120, 123, 127, 129, 131-3, 143, 150, 153-4, 203, 218, 232, 242

configurations   126-8, 132, 218, 240, 242

consistency   65, 76, 78, 81, 93, 147, 159

context   1, 44, 51, 65, 82, 88, 123-5, 239

Continual Service Improvement   8-9, 51, 56, 64, 79, 109, 192, 211-15, 220, 222, 237

continuity   28-9, 57, 100, 102, 104-5

contracts   66-7, 69, 72, 75, 79, 96, 100, 107, 239, 247

costs   20-3, 33-4, 39, 45-8, 55, 73, 77, 86, 111, 120-2, 127, 131, 140, 159, 162-3, 242

CSI (Continuous Service Improvement)   31, 56, 214, 222, 237

customer perspective   48, 53, 83

D

databases   41, 125-6, 130, 193, 242, 244

demand   32, 34, 48-53, 55, 58, 85-7, 89, 157

Demand Management   6, 44, 47-53, 89, 117, 228, 243

departments   14, 65, 70, 115, 160, 169, 173, 199-200

dependencies   81, 117, 181, 228, 240

deploy   142-4, 152, 245

deployment   41, 80, 123, 143-6, 148-9, 173, 205

design   12, 25, 28, 32, 48, 51, 53, 58, 60, 62-3, 71, 76, 96, 111, 173, 213-14

detection   98, 112-13, 131, 178

diagnosis   85, 92, 98, 184, 189, 193, 196

disaster   100-1, 103-4

disruptions   14, 16, 87, 92, 95, 98-100, 118, 166, 173, 179-81, 186, 209, 228-9, 236, 240, 245

DML (Definitive Media Library)   144-5, 154, 232

downtime   94, 97, 118, 229-30, 239

duplication   41, 69-70

E

effectiveness   69, 78, 82, 99, 127, 133, 137, 142, 150, 156, 175, 190-1, 198, 244

employees   50-1, 136, 247

errors   123, 133, 192-5, 208, 234

Event Management   8, 94, 176-9, 184, 207, 210, 236

events   27, 50, 53, 74, 100, 172, 176-80, 189, 209-10, 235-6, 243

execution   14, 50, 110, 147, 156, 172, 203, 205

F

Financial Management   6, 15, 44-7, 53, 59, 117, 214, 225, 228, 239-43, 246

framework   1, 11, 16-19, 28, 68, 107-9, 215-16

functions   19-20, 25-7, 30, 51, 60, 76, 94-6, 143, 154, 160-1, 205, 210, 217, 225, 227, 248

G

gaps   68, 73, 163, 213-14

H

hardware   12, 22, 39, 47, 58, 89, 130, 142, 144, 242-3, 245-6
hours   38, 95-6, 176, 187
HYPE   57-8, 116, 152, 207, 221

I

implementation   25, 40-1, 78, 109-10, 139-40, 149, 161, 164, 184, 192, 202, 233, 245
improvements   1, 17, 60, 65, 72-3, 98-9, 120, 131, 135, 166, 171, 173, 205, 212-15, 217,
  221-2
Incident Management   8, 15, 27, 175, 179-81, 183-5, 191-3, 196, 209, 235, 243-5, 248
incident records   127, 180, 187, 195, 248
incidents   27-8, 32, 50, 59, 85, 92, 97, 112, 145, 181-2, 184-94, 207-8, 234, 242-3, 245,
  247-8
Information Security Management   7, 64, 106, 110, 112, 202-3, 230
infrastructure   40, 54, 88-90, 100, 112, 120, 128, 140, 158-9, 169-70, 172, 177-8, 181-2,
  208-9, 234-6, 239-41
initiatives   42-3, 46, 143, 219
interfaces   34, 55, 62-3, 75, 81, 129, 135, 173, 178, 192, 200, 202-3, 213, 215
investments   17, 41, 65, 77, 123, 220, 246
ISP (Internet Service Provider)   35-9, 115
IT Service Continuity Management (ITSCM)   7, 64, 93, 100, 102, 104, 117, 119, 228, 230,
  240, 248
ITSM (IT Service Management)   1, 6, 10-19, 22, 28, 34, 68, 74, 106, 143, 172, 174, 195,
  211-12, 242, 244-7

K

Knowledge Management   7, 122-5, 244
Known Errors   28, 165, 193-6, 207-8, 234, 244
KPIs (Key Performance Indicators)   217-18, 242, 244

L

library   16, 130, 144, 243-4
license   24, 28, 35, 43, 50, 75, 78, 82, 89, 91, 93, 97, 102, 108, 111-12, 131-2
lifecycle   28-9, 31, 41, 63, 76, 79, 126-7, 130, 132, 174, 202, 220, 239, 241-5
locations   122, 147, 161-2, 243

M

maintenance   79, 81, 92-3, 96, 101, 110, 209, 236
market space   21, 34, 43-4, 55
mechanisms   80-1, 136, 190, 200-1, 247
metrics   63, 95, 99, 142, 167, 217-18, 221, 244
modifications   90, 135, 202-3, 207, 232, 241
money   11, 20, 23, 40, 46, 74-5, 240, 242
monitoring   89, 167-8, 172, 176, 178, 216, 222, 237, 240
MTBF (Mean Time Between Failures)   95, 97-9, 118, 230
MTBSI (Mean Time Between Service Incidents)   95, 98-9, 118, 230
MTRS (Mean Time to Restore Service)   95-9, 118, 230

O

objectives   7-8, 13, 15-16, 49, 62, 74-5, 80-1, 85, 92, 108-9, 120, 122, 127, 161, 213, 217-18
OGC   24, 28, 35, 43, 50, 75, 78, 82, 89, 91, 93, 97, 102, 108, 111-12, 124
OLAs (Operational Level Agreement)   66-7, 71-2, 99, 108, 118, 229, 245, 247
Operations Management   8, 20, 169, 171-2, 207
ownership   20, 22, 26, 168, 239

P

partners   10-11, 61, 76, 79, 106-7, 227
pathways   9, 249-50
patterns   25, 34, 49, 52, 56
perceptions   22, 87, 92, 214
performance   12, 36, 40, 53-4, 56, 65, 85, 88-90, 94, 167, 176-7, 214, 216-18, 227-8, 239
person   2, 19-21, 24, 130, 136, 242, 247-8
perspectives   6, 11-13, 45, 61, 83, 106, 112-13, 119, 133, 214, 227, 230
phases   29, 31-2, 44, 57, 64, 120, 146, 148, 156, 179, 211
planning   55, 68, 100, 104, 108, 129, 131, 182, 239, 246
policies   20, 24, 55, 60, 78, 83, 101, 107, 109-11, 129, 200, 202, 216, 226, 245
portfolio   41, 43, 211
Problem Management   8, 94, 117, 178, 180, 182, 190, 192-5, 198, 208, 228, 234-5, 244-5, 248
problems   4, 28, 48, 54, 131, 145, 192-7, 208-9, 234-5, 242, 244-5, 248
process owners   20-1, 24, 213, 218

Q

quality   10, 12, 14, 22, 32, 34, 48, 56, 69, 76, 114, 122, 127, 159, 166-7, 243-4

R

RACI Model   6, 26-7
recovery   95, 97, 105, 131, 145, 184, 189, 228
reduction   99, 110, 112, 242-3
relationships   8, 16, 29, 51, 66, 68-9, 71, 74-5, 78-9, 82, 98, 118, 128, 130, 140-1, 241-2
Release and Deployment Management   7, 143, 145, 154, 232-3
releases   16, 32, 121, 131, 142-8, 151, 197, 209, 218, 231, 235, 240, 246
reliability   56, 92, 94-7, 99, 239
Request Fulfillment   8, 181, 199, 201
requests   55, 123, 127, 133, 137, 161-2, 167, 199-201, 208, 221, 234, 246
resources   1, 14, 16, 20, 23, 40, 42, 46, 55, 63, 72, 85-6, 88, 96, 102, 170
responsibilities   10, 12, 20, 24-7, 51, 65, 67, 69, 72, 90, 98, 104-5, 113, 140-1, 147-8, 215-16
RFCs (Request for Changes)   55, 127, 136-9, 141-2, 203, 208, 221, 234, 246-7
risks   6, 14, 20-2, 33, 40-3, 48, 55, 73, 94, 120, 123, 134, 137, 139-40, 146, 163
ROI (Return on Investment)   44, 205, 220, 246
roles   10, 12, 20-2, 24-7, 44, 47, 51, 59, 64, 67, 75, 160, 169-73, 215-16, 225-6, 229
root cause   180, 182, 192-3, 195, 245

S

thresholds   136, 179, 181
tools   1, 5, 12, 17, 20, 24, 26, 63, 109, 113, 123, 125-6, 145, 157, 204-5, 215-16
transfer   47, 148-9, 188
tuning   89-90, 117, 205, 228

U

unavailability   94-5, 99, 118, 229
understanding   1, 22, 31, 41-2, 45, 49-50, 55, 57, 72-3, 94-5, 122, 124, 134
utility   38-9, 55, 57, 60, 226-7

V

value   1, 3, 10-11, 19-20, 22-3, 25, 35-8, 40, 45-9, 53, 55, 57-8, 60, 65, 74-5, 220
VBFs (Vital Business Function)   96, 102, 240, 248
version   1, 5, 16-17, 28-30, 48
vision   213-14, 217, 222, 237

W

warranty   2, 38-9, 48, 51, 55-7, 60, 226-7
wisdom   124-5, 153, 231
workarounds   165, 193, 196, 207, 244, 248

LaVergne, TN USA
18 August 2010
193817LV00004B/10/P